Country Five

Raymond Rush

Illustrated by
Sheila Hine

With my very best wishes,

The chapters in this book originally appeared as monthly
articles in the Town & Country Post by whose kind permission
they have been reprinted and revised. Many of the articles
have also been featured on television and radio.

Raymond Rush.

CHURNET VALLEY BOOKS
1 King Street, Leek, Staffordshire 01538 399033
www.leekbooks.co.uk
© Raymond Rush, Sheila Hine and Churnet Valley Books 2008
ISBN 9781 904546573

**CONTENTS OF COUNTRYWISE
ONE, TWO, THREE & FOUR
ARE LISTED ON PAGE 128**

Contents

... And just like before, everything is nicely 'pigeon-holed'
- see article 153 in Countrywise Four.

156 May Gamekeepers
'WITHOUT GAME THERE WOULD BE NO GAMEKEEPERS'

Have you ever been startled by the explosive sound of whirring wings as a frightened pheasant soars upwards to the safety of the open sky just in front of you.

Or watched in wonder as a covey of partridge bask in their dust bowls on the headland of a freshly ploughed corn stubble. Then admired the symmetry of their flight when flushed as they alternatively flap and glide on down-curved wings, skimming just above the surface of the field, rising only fractionally above the crest of the opposite hedge.

It is right that we should relish those rare magical moments for in a matter of months many of these beautiful birds may be hanging from hooks in butchers shops.

But before you start to complain that they shouldn't be shot for sport, remember that if there were no shooting syndicates there would soon be no gamekeepers and probably no pheasants or partridges left to admire. For the vast majority of game birds that adorn our countryside have been hand reared by him.

His cottage snuggles in its clearing in surrounding woodland, sheltered from penetrating winds and isolated from the gaze of inquisitive mortals. Around it are clustered a motley collection of sheds, lean-to's, huts and kennels that house the tools of his trade, the animals and birds of his livelihood and some of the macabre results of his labours.

He wears the engrained face of a person who is outdoors in all weathers, is mentally and physically alert and is seldom sick or sorry. His isolated lifestyle gives him a deep understanding of the ways and wiles of the animals, birds (and people) in his area and as a general rule he keeps that knowledge strictly to himself.

The stout ash stick that he carries has many uses. It aids his balance when the going underfoot is rough or slippery, it brushes aside the brambles, will quickly dispatch a rat caught in a trap and remind an errant dog to come to heel.

His main purpose in life is to keep his employer(s) happy. To do this he must raise a sufficient number of game, mainly pheasants and partridge to provide shooting during an allocated number of days during the autumn and winter, which is certainly not as easy as it sounds.

In the squire's day, the keeper would have had one or two under keepers to help him. He now has to achieve a similar output on his own so both means and methods have had to change.

Apart from the weather, especially thunderstorms which will drown newly-hatched chicks, the other main cause of loss among his stock is vermin. Among which he includes poachers, not the casual 'one-off' local chap who takes the occasional bird to feed his family, but the unscrupulous city gangs who can clear a wood in a night. Against them he wages a constant war of wits.

In addition to his Jack Russell or other terrier he maintains and regularly inspects a network of underground trapping areas throughout his domain to catch rats, stoats and weasels. As he says 'a trap eats nothing and never minds waiting'. He also has to be on constant alert for larger four-footed fiends - feral cats that have been dumped and are scouring the woods for food. Also this year a scourge of mangy urban foxes that have been caught in towns and let loose in the countryside to fend for themselves in a strange environment, devoid of dustbins, the former source of most of their food.

Grey squirrels or tree rats as they are also called can devastate young birds if their numbers are not kept under strict control. Crafty jay and magpie populations are reduced by using cage traps with a decoy bird, but the cunning carrion crow generally has to be shot to be sure he doesn't plunder the partridge and pheasant chicks.

Most of these pests end up exhibited on the 'Gamekeeper's Gibbet' - the side of one of his wooden sheds. Or as with moles, dangling along a stretch of barbed wire. The object of this exercise is not to act as a dire warning to other rodents or birds of prey as many people believe, but to let his employer and neighbouring farmers see that he is doing the job he is being paid for, keeping the vermin under control.

Preparations for the new season start before the old season finishes. The last shoot at the end of January is usually for 'cocks only,' to reduce the number of cock pheasants, for by nature each cock bird will try to gather together a harem of up to 10 hens.

During February, March and April the gamekeeper tries to catch as many cocks and hens as he can. About six hens are penned with each cock bird to fertilise the eggs. The keeper often swaps cock birds with other shoots to prevent in-breeding.

In late spring, until a few years ago, the keeper would visit all the farms in the area buying up broody hens at £1 a piece, each hen would sit a clutch of a dozen or so eggs in a coop.

Our local keeper specially favoured our silky bantams as they were light in weight, sat tight, did not trample or crack the eggs and were excellent mothers when the chicks hatched some 25 days later. Nowadays 'modern' battery hens have had the broodiness bred out of them, which means the keeper has to collect and hatch the eggs in an incubator or buy day-old chicks from special game hatcheries.

If he wished to obtain extra eggs the gamekeeper would hunt around the grassy bogs of the hedge bank. There, in a shallow earth scrape lightly lined with grass he might find the olive green eggs of our native partridge or the creamy brown, grey spotted clutch of the red legged or French partridge hidden under a covering of dead grass and leaves - until she starts to sit early in May.

Left to her own devices the French partridge sometimes lays two separate clutches of about 15 eggs at roughly the same time. She sits and incubates the one, while her husband hatches the other, how's that for sharing the chores and raising a family in marital harmony?

With pheasants it is only the hen who sits on her brown eggs, the cock is too busy strutting around, displaying his plumage and crowing about his achievements! In the wild both pheasants and partridge poults live on greenery, insects and later seeds, and they are able to fly at about two weeks.

Hand reared chicks are soon transferred to rearing pens in the woods which are sited on fresh ground each year to reduce disease. There they are slowly introduced to a wider freedom with wire netting protection from foxes.

Because they are fed daily they remain tame until they start being shot at. And of course many other species of garden and woodland birds take advantage of and benefit from this supply of free food, it helps them survive the rigours of Winter.

Although partridge shooting officially begins on the first of September and pheasants on the 1st of October they are often left for an extra week or two to 'plump' up a bit.

The shoot is run like a military operation with the keeper acting as commander-in-chief and in strict control. He has to be, for guns are dangerous weapons, especially in the hands of wealthy novices, some of whom tend to think they can ignore the rules.

On the day of the shoot everything is done according to a pre-arranged plan organised in advance by the keeper. Early in the morning he dispatches a couple of 'stoppers' to each wood, these men or boys try to prevent the game leaving the area. He has already put out numbered markers in each of the 'drives' where the 'guns' are to be positioned.

At around 9.30 to 10am after a warming sherry or whisky, the eight to 10 'guns' draw lots for their number and are allocated their positions usually behind the cover of a hedge. The keeper then assembles the dozen or so 'beaters' into a line on the opposite side of the wood with a 'flagman' at each end.

Starting at the command of the keeper or his whistle they walk forward through the undergrowth, tapping it with their sticks, flushing the birds who run in front of them to the further edge of the wood.

There is it hoped they will rise and fly towards the 'guns' hidden behind the hedge at the far side of the field. The flagmen at either end try to stop them veering off to the left or the right. The guns shoot, some birds are shot and fall, some rise vertically then plummet like a stone, some crash land on one wing and start to run away - 'runners.' If the guns have to stop to reload then a great many birds manage to escape which is why on some of the bigger shoots the 'gun' has two guns, while he is firing one gun his assistant is loading the other so very few possible shots are missed.

At the end of the drive, dogs are sent to pick up the fallen birds and the keeper sends his trained retrievers after the 'runners.' The dead birds are put into the game cart where they hang in regimented rows by their necks. The guns move to their next numbered places and the beaters line up to walk through a field of waist high kale. If it is wet they all get saturated.

After this drive it may well be time for dinner.

The 'guns' go indoors at the hall, the keepers or a farmers for refreshments, washed down with wine or spirits; whilst the beaters shelter in the buildings outside and have their sandwiches, flask of coffee or cans of beer. All too soon the keeper signals the start of the next drive.

By about mid afternoon the light is fading and a

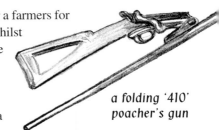

a folding '410'
poacher's gun

halt is called. The 'guns' select a brace of game for themselves if they wish, the rest will go to the game room at the hall to hang for a few days and then be sold to defray some of the costs. The 'guns' thank the gamekeeper for his organisation of a successful shoot and when departing usually leave a 'note of appreciation' in his hand to help supplement his meagre wage. The wet, thorn torn and weary beaters are paid off by the keeper and told when their services are next required. Most are well satisfied with their reward and gratefully thank the keeper. And so it continues periodically until the 'cocks only' shoot at the end of the season, on 31st January.

The gamekeeper is generally on good terms with the local farmers, a few may even shoot; the 'shoot' certainly shoots over their land and the farmer helps by keeping an eye on the game.

At Christmas and the end of the season the farmer is usually given a brace of birds as a 'token of gratitude,' for which the keeper generally gains a 'tip' and sometimes also a 'tipple.'

Shooting certainly isn't a cheap sport, I once heard it described as follows: 'You pay £1,000 a year to join a club which allows you to fire a ten penny cartridge from a £1,000 gun to kill a bird that has cost £5 to rear, and when you sell it you will only get £1 for it, that's shooting.' An even older quote is: 'Up goes a guinea, bang goes sixpence, down comes half a crown

But remember without the income from shooting syndicates the gamekeeper would soon become an endangered species, vermin would increase, and many of our songbirds decrease. Pheasants and partridge would soon be on the verge of extinction and many of our small woods, plantations and copses, no longer needed for cover, would disappear.

And that is the GAMEKEEPER'S story!

157 June Canals
'SLEEPY CANALS WERE A QUICK ROUTE FOR CARGO'

Whether they are passing through the centre of our towns and cities or the backwaters of our countryside, canals present a picture of peacefulness and solitude.

They exude an atmosphere of tranquil calm and gentleness, tucked just far enough away from the hustle and bustle of modern life.

They are an almost undisturbed haven for wildlife, walkers and the many fishermen who patiently maintain their lonely vigil at intervals along the grassy banks. The silence is only broken by the sound of an occasional fish plopping out of the surface or the surface being disturbed by the chug, chug, chugging of a passing pleasure boat.

Yet only a few years ago that vast network of our canals were a green, slimy, smelly and stagnant mess, choked with weeds. The majority were putrid rubbish-strewn dumping grounds for the discarded items of our throwaway society, old bicycles, broken prams, shopping trolleys and 'banger' cars.

The restoration that has taken place is largely the result of enthusiastic voluntary workers who have dredged the deeps, cleared the channels, repaired the lock gates, painted the posts and tidied the towpaths so that they are once again a credit to our countryside and a reminder of their former essential role in the development of our industrial heritage.

England was the first country in the world to become 'industrial'. From about 1750 the 'Revolution' began as people started to leave the countryside in drifts and later in droves, to work in the new mills and manufactories (factories) that were springing up wherever there was a sufficient head of water to turn the water wheel to drive them.

It was more profitable to spin cotton than to grind corn, consequently wages were higher than on the farms and therefore a greater lure.

For the first time in their lives workers had money to spend which led to an increased demand for goods, which in turn meant an ever increasing movement of raw materials as well as finished products.

Sailing boats conveyed their cargoes around sea ports and, where the rivers had been widened and deepened, to a few ports inland. But there the cargo had to be unloaded onto slow, cumbersome carts or pack horses and taken overland to the destination.

Similarly the finished article had to make the return journey by rutted roads and narrow tracks back to the sea ports and thence around England by sail.

Vast quantities were on the move; cotton bales from Liverpool to the mills in Manchester, Leeds and towns en route; coal from Lancashire and the Midlands; china clay from Cornwall to Stoke on Trent and the finished products back to ports, iron goods from the Black Country, and so the list continued.

Industrialists eager to expand their businesses were frustrated by the slow and costly transport system. How could they overcome the handicap of our poor roads? Which is where the canals came in; but like many things which we think are relatively recent and typically English, their origin goes way back into history and to distant lands.

Over 500 years Before Christ (BC) the Egyptians built a canal to link the Red Sea with the Nile. I'm not sure whether it was the same one, but during my spell in the forces I was stationed on the banks of one, along which flowed not only graceful sailing dhows but also dead dogs and donkeys, and they called it the 'Sweet Water Canal'!

The Grand Canal of China was over 800 miles long and took 600 years to complete (until 800AD (Anno Domini). In 1487 an engineer called Leonardo da Vinci invented double swinging gates with a mitred centre for controlling the flow of water instead of the vicious guillotine type of sluice that had been used before.

Because the water was impounded when the gates were shut -locked - they were originally called 'Pound Locks' now, just 'Locks'. They were introduced into England in the reign of Queen Elizabeth I on a canal that linked the River Exe to Exeter.

Monks were renowned for widening, deepening, strengthening and straightening rivers to aid 'navigation', from which our words for canal makers ' navigators' and 'navvy' derive.

In 1699 the French completed an overland waterway between the Mediterranean and the Atlantic to save ships sailing all the way around Spain. It was 150 miles long, had 100 locks, 3 aqueducts and straddled hills 300 feet high.

It so inspired the industrialist Francis Egerton, the 3rd Duke of Bridgewater that he employed a self educated millwright called James Brindley to construct an 18 mile canal between his coal mines at Worsley and the centre of Manchester.

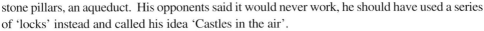

This canal went deep into the hill to the heart of the mines at Worsley. It crossed the river Irwell in a clay lined iron trough which stood on stone pillars, an aqueduct. His opponents said it would never work, he should have used a series of 'locks' instead and called his idea 'Castles in the air'.

However, when it opened in 1761 it did work, so successfully in fact that it halved the cost of carting coal and made the Duke of Bridgewater one of the richest men in England!

Such was its success that other canal companies were soon formed to join the four main rivers of the Thames, Severn, Trent and Humber and thus the cities of London, Bristol, Hull, Manchester and Liverpool and many others en route.

The main criteria for building a canal were:

1. To make sure there was sufficient water available to fill it when completed and maintain it in operation, especially during dry summer months and if there were locks on the system. This usually involved damming a stream and creating a reservoir. Rudyard Lake in Staffordshire is an example.

2. To dig out a trench of the required size, using the surplus soil to strengthen the banks, create a towpath and fill in any slight hollows. Making 'cuttings' through small hills and 'embankments' over shallow valleys.

3. Make everything waterproof particularly in free draining soils like sand and chalk. This was achieved by lining the whole area with several inches of 'puddled' clay, a clay and water mix, which became impervious. The bottom of the former mill pond on my farm was waterproofed this way.

This 'boom' in canal construction lasted about 70 years until 1830 by which time some 4,000 miles of inland waterways had been completed. One particular period of four years from 1790 was known as 'canal mania', when Parliament authorised the building of 81 new canals.

It seemed that everyone wanted to get in on the act and own shares in canal companies. Some of the earlier investors certainly did very well out of it, but many later ones got their fingers badly burned and went bankrupt if the company ran out of money before the canal was completed. Several canals had to wait for funds from some other source before they could be finished, a few never were!

As everything was done by hand canal construction was a lengthy process involving hordes of hard working, hard drinking, hard swearing 'navvygators' as James Brindley wrote it, which is why they were called 'navvies'.

These armies of labourers were also known as the 'pick and shovel' brigade after the tools they used. Like a plague of locusts they were widely feared as they swarmed across the country digging out their earthen dykes, filling wheelbarrows to dump the soil on the banks beside them or into carts to carry it further away. While in their leisure time many an innocent young lady fell victim to their advances!

To keep the cost of construction as low as possible early pioneers followed the natural contours of the countryside.

I used to walk across this curious bridge at Woodseaves in Staffordshire when I was courting

Their canals were longer but they had fewer locks. As canal builders learned how to overcome obstacles their followers, such as Thomas Telford, kept to a more direct route, arguing that the extra initial expense in building costs was justified by the time saved on every journey.

One factor which is not always recognised is that apart from the 'navvies' the canals provided a tremendous amount of work for many other groups of craftsmen. Foresters, sawyers and hauliers were required to produce vast quantities of timber so that carpenters could construct hundreds of lock gates and boat builders thousands of canal craft.

Foundry men and ironworkers in the Black Country cast sections for the new iron-bridges, aqueduct troughs and bollards. Blacksmiths supplied wrought ironwork sluices, lock paddles and numerous smaller items for boats; quarrymen and stonemasons built the structures surrounding each lock and sluice; brickmakers, bricklayers and builders erected lock-keepers' and boatmen's houses.

Canals were such an important part of our 'Industrial Revolution' their story will be continued in the next article.

158 July More Canals
'INGENIOUS ENGINEERS TOOK THEIR CANALS THROUGH HILL AND VALE'

Until the coming of the canals 'engineers' were mainly military men employed to construct weapons of war. Now for almost the first time they were civilians and so were called 'civil engineers'.

The three main tasks they had to tackle were to build 'locks' to provide 'steps' in the water level, 'tunnels' to go through larger hills and 'aqueducts' to span valleys. I will deal with each task separately and give a few examples.

Raising and lowering a boat to another level generally required a 'lock'. In order to reduce maintenance the sides and base were built of stone.

Both ends of the lock could be sealed by a pair of gates that met in the middle with a mitred edge, which pointed to the higher level like an arrowhead. Each gate was hinged on a heelpost of a rounded tree trunk which fitted into a recess in the wall, and was held in place with a socket at the bottom and an iron loop at the top.

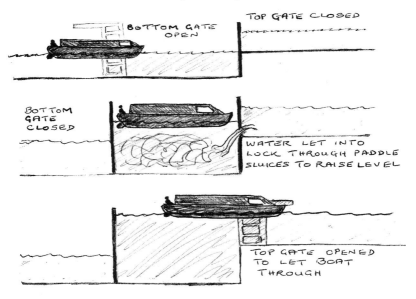

When the gates were shut the water pressure sealed the central mitred joint and the heelpost hinge so that no water could pass. Along the top of each gate an extra thick baulk of timber extended over the banks, it served four purposes:
- As one of the main gate beams.
- The overhang acted as a lever to help open and close the gate.
- The overhang also helped to counterbalance the weight of the gate.
- Being broad it made a useful footbridge to cross the canal - a widened walkway, with protective railings sometimes added to help prevent accidents.

At the bottom of each gate were one or two, three foot square, paddle sluices (or in

windlass

culverts in the lock wall). They were screwed up and down by a square ended bar, turned by a removable windlass.

To lift a boat to a higher level it entered the lower lock. The open gates were closed behind it - as were the paddle sluices at the bottom of each gate. The paddle sluices in the upper pair of gates were opened and about 26,000 gallons of water from the higher part of the canal gradually filled the lock.

When, and only when, the water level in the lock was the same as that in the upper canal could the gates be opened, before that the water pressure was too great. Contrary to many people's belief the gates only opened to let the *boat* pass through, *not the water*. Each gate swung back to fit snugly into a recess in its side wall so that it was not damaged by passing traffic.

A boat 'going down' entered the full lock, the gates and sluices were closed behind it. The sluices were opened in the gates leading to the lower canal letting the water out of the lock. When the levels were equal the gates could be opened and the boat went on its way.

On average it took about 20 minutes to pass through a lock, a simple way of overcoming gradients - until you had to do it all day, as in the famous 'Cheshire locks' where there were 30 to be negotiated in 13 miles on the 'Trent & Mersey' between Stoke on Trent & Middlewich. It is known as 'Heartbreak Hill'.

Of course locks impeded the smooth passage of boats and caused 'bottlenecks'. To try to prevent that some locks were doubled in width to accommodate two boats at a time, others were lit by gaslight so that cargoes could pass throughout the night to avoid traffic jams. Two other methods of altering levels were:

1. To haul the boat overland on a special inclined railway;
2. To lift or lower the barge in a dock of water. This was the principle of the Anderton lift at Northwich where originally one boat was lifted fifty feet to the upper section of the Trent & Mersey canal, its weight being compensated by another boat being lowered the fifty feet into the River Weaver. This system has since been replaced by electric motors.

To overcome the problem of high hills the best long term solution was to dig a tunnel right through and come out at the same level on the other side. For strength the tunnels were lined with brick but were often too narrow to incorporate a towpath.

To move the boat through, the men lay on their backs and pushed against the walls or roof with an action known as 'legging it' - at about 2mph. Meanwhile the towing horse had to be walked around or over the hill, but as the boatmen often had to wait for it on the other side some took the horse aboard for the ride through the tunnel instead.

Later on a few tunnels were fitted with a steam driven continuous hawser or an electric tug fed by overhead wires as in the 'Harecastle' tunnel just north of Stoke-on-Trent.

From 1803 one of the most famous aqueducts in the world was the 'Wonder of Wales'. It spanned the Vale of Llangollen at Pont-Cy-Syllte, 120 feet above the Dee. Built by Thomas Telford this 'Stream in the sky' rested on gigantic stone piers. Although it was such a difficult and dangerous project, which took over ten years to build, there was only ever one accident.

'Narrowboats' that plied the canals were 7ft wide, 70 feet long and could carry 30 tons. Apart from occasionally having to be pulled by the boatmen and his family during emergencies, they were usually hauled by a single horse or two donkeys, who had their grazing provided free of charge at the side of the towpath.

A fact which is not often recognised is that if the boat were towed from the front it would veer 'straight' into the bank, to compensate, the rope was fastened to a bollard or mast about a quarter the way along the boat. The tiller with its long curved handle also helped to steer a correct course.

Many bridges and short tunnel entrances bear the scars of a century or more of canal traffic where deep grooves have been worn onto the stonework by hempen tow ropes.

One very interesting bridge, called a 'turnover', allowed the horse to cross to the opposite towpath without unhitching the boat simply by going up and over the bridge before passing underneath it on the far side - very ingenious.

Canal companies owned the waterways but the boatmen owned their boats and paid a tariff to use the canals. In the early days boatmen and boys lived ashore with their family, often in small houses supplied by the canal company. But as competition increased with the arrival of the railways, rates were forced down, boatmen could no longer afford the luxury of a land base, so families lived aboard. There in cramped conditions only about seven feet square the boatmen and his wife often raised a large family

The planning of the area would put modern 'bed-sits' to shame.

On the left was a cooking stove and a food and crockery cupboard with a hinged lid that let down to act as a table. Across the back was a double bunk, on the right a side-bed, used for seating by day and where the children slept at night. For extra space and safety small children played in a collapsible mesh pen on deck when it was fine during the day.

Generally speaking boatpeople were happy people, they loved bright colours and painted their cabin doors, boat panels and most moveable items of hardware with traditional designs of castles and roses known as 'barge work'.

In spite of the lack of washing facilities and frequent filthy or dusty cargoes the pride in the smartness of their vessels also extended to themselves. The ladies knitted, sewed and were often skillful at embroidery and crochet work.

Canalside communities sprang up, shops to sell food and wares and Navigation Inns to supply victuals to the boatpeople, many of whom plied the same length of canal the whole of their working life.

Ironically it was the very skills learned by the civil engineers in constructing the canals that helped to hasten their end, for from 1840 the railway fast became the new mode of transport. Just like the canals they required a level base, cuttings, embankments, tunnels and viaducts. Soon the rail network covered those parts of the country that the canals could not reach. Farmers sent their milk and perishable products to the towns by this new and quicker method - the train. It wasn't that the canal traffic suddenly ceased, it didn't, it carried on for a long while but didn't expand any further. The railways took over most of the new and often more lucrative trade. Many of the canal companies were taken over by the railways and slowly went into decline.

Now the remaining narrow boats have been transformed into holiday homes for pleasure cruising. Even the thriving railways that replaced the canal traffic have been superceded by road transport and aeroplanes.

Waterways, railways, motorways, airways, I wonder what will be next - space ways? Or will we return to those slow, quiet and peaceful waterways of yesteryear - I doubt it.

159 August Playtimes Past
'....AND MY MEMORIES OF THEM'

It was Lot 162 at a local auction of household goods. I was intrigued and stood looking at it for ages.

To most people it was just another picture, a large print of an old masterpiece by Peter Brueghel, painted about 400 years ago, depicting a scene in a foreign town in a bygone age. But what struck me was that there were children and grown ups playing the very same games and doing the things that I remembered vividly as a youngster. It brought back so many memories that just for old times sake I left a bid of a fiver on it with the auctioneer.

I recall that either at school or when my many cousins came to visit we would play 'Pick-a-back' usually called 'piggy back' and have races up and down the playground or lawn. Then quite suddenly the same game would turn into a medieval contest of knights on horseback trying to topple one another off. When we grew older and more daring we 'battled' astride our 'horse's' shoulders.

Almost every child had a 'hoop', either an iron one made by the local blacksmith or a wooden one that had become detached from a barrel. With these we would run races propelling and guiding them with a short stick.

I remember my proper iron handled loop was forever getting lost, it was usually found in the same place that I had discarded it when playing! We also learned to throw the hoops several yards forward and with back-spin make them return to us.

A steep grassy slope was always a favourite haunt. We would run down at an incredible speed, do 'head over heels' or lie down and 'roly-poly', rotating rapidly to the bottom often colliding with someone coming up.

On level ground we practised walking on our hands or performing 'cartwheels', then tiring of that hold onto one another's tails in a snake like procession of 'follow my leader'.

Wherever the leader went everyone followed, through gaps in the hedge, up the thatching ladder, down the straw stack on the other side into a mattress of loose straw, in and out of the cowshed doors, through the hay lofts. The older children helping and encouraging the less able.

On cooler days someone was 'It' and after a count of fifty would chase after and catch us all, putting us in a den, prison or hell depending on which version of the game was in vogue at the time. The last to be caught became the new 'It' (or 'He').

A variant was to have two people 'on', prisoners would be encircled and captured by a long rope held between them, once caught you held on to the rope and helped to catch others, it sometimes became a bit cumbersome but it was great fun.

Any toddler getting too tired or feeling poorly might well be carried home by two older ones clasping hand to wrist making an impromptu square seat. A very simple hand game was placing one on top of the other, withdrawing the bottom one and putting it on top.

Another was hiding a marble in one hand behind your back then presenting the two clenched hands in front and asking 'Which hand is it in?' And of course speaking of marbles there were a dozen different ways of playing them; getting them into a hole, knocking opponents marbles out of the circle or just simply hitting them to claim them.

Marbles could also be rolled through numbered 'doorways' cut into a length of board the winner obtained the highest score. Skittles were stood up and knocked over, mine were painted to look like soldiers and we had wooden balls which soon became anything but round as pieces broke off them.

Although 'caps' were an official part of our school outfit, it was seldom I wore mine. Apart from being carried in my cycle saddlebag in case of wet weather, we did use them for playing a couple of games. The 'leader' would skim his cap just above the ground, the winner was the one who spun his nearest to it. The second was throwing a cap onto a short stick pushed into the ground.

We also had 'sword fights' with sticks, which continued until one of us got our knuckles bruised, a less hazardous version was using thin whippy sticks as 'rapiers'. Early in the year there was always a craze for 'whipping tops'. They came in many different shapes and sizes, one, the most popular was the 'goats head' which looked like a mushroom and was widely known as a 'window breaker'.

Most farms and cottages had at least one old beer barrel, used for a rabbit hutch or housing broody hens. We used to sit astride them and have a 'sack-fight' - same as a pillow fight but our hessian bags were stuffed with hay.

We would also try to walk on smaller barrels to move them along, but this was a real balancing act. I think it was an Uncle that made me my first pair of 'stilts', from two blocks of wood screwed to two broom handles. I struggled for ages to get the knack of jumping on and walking off.

Soon most of my friends had a pair and we used to see who could go the farthest without falling off. A similar idea was two syrup tins held tightly against your feet as you walked by a loop of string in each hand.

I suppose boys will be boys and one of our favourite games was playing 'catch' through the branches of a copse of trees. Apart from being caught you were considered 'out' if your feet touched the ground.

We used a multitude of springy elm saplings to swing from tree to tree, imitating our screen hero of that time 'Tarzan'. A single rope suspended from a very high branch made a marvellous swing. We sat or stood on a bundle of knots tied in the end and could travel in a wide arc and also spin around.

This was a great feature of our farmyard swing, twisting the ropes round and round then sitting and watching the world whiz by, when it stopped, getting off and not being able to walk in a straight line for the dizziness.

If a tree blew down it wasn't sawn up immediately as today. A stout plank would be carried to it and we would spend ages 'see-sawing', reaching heights considered dangerous to the 'tiny tots' see-saw equivalents of today.

If I was on my own I could still see-saw using a heavy bough. The long thick heavy end compensating for my weight on the lighter end, my little legs acting as springs. Running along the tree trunk, especially if it had been raining, taught composure and balance.

All told I must have spent hours doing somersaults around the single iron pipe that acted as a guard rail to the gurgling stream beneath. It was a favourite stopping place for us on the way to school and homeward bound.

By coincidence many years later we moved to within 100 yards of it and because we didn't have a mains water supply, one of my regular tasks was to fill the swinging two wheeled galvanised water cart from that very stream to water our large flock of free range hens. Before or after the filling I'd sometimes sneak in a somersault - providing no one was watching - for by then I had grown into a rather shy teenager!

Running full tilt at a wall, up it and twisting backwards took a lot of skill and courage. I could never manage that one but our ringleader at school could do it every time, and how we envied him.

On the farm we seldom stopped to climb over a five bar gate, we just put our hands on the top bar and vaulted over. My dad showed my children how to do it when he was in his fifties and how to jump the wooden garden seat. Although I feel I'm getting a bit too stiff in the joints to actually do those thing now, I still enjoy thinking about all the wonderful games we used to play and things we used to get up to in the heyday of our youth.

And if you're wondering how I remember all these items that were included in that picture - well much to my surprise it was knocked down to me and I have it in front of me as I write. I think you'll agree that the memories it has recalled made it well worth that fiver!

160 September Retirement
'MICHAELMAS - A TIME TO END AND A TIME TO BEGIN AGAIN'

I suppose in most people's life there comes a time to say 'enough is enough'. For over forty years I have been doing it twice a day with hardly a break, so my wife and I have decided that this Michaelmas is the time to start to wind down and begin to ease the workload. It was a difficult decision to make after taking many factors into account.

But more of that in a minute, first a few items about this largely forgotten season of the year.

The introduction of the Harvest Festival 150 years ago has diminished much of the importance of 29th September, the feast of St. Michael. Most people only know of its existence today because of the tall dark blue daisy like flower that blooms at this season of the year the 'Michaelmas daisy', often grey with mildew (rather like me).

However, did you know that you should never eat blackberries after 29th September - Michaelmas? According to Chapter 12 of the Revelation of St John the Divine there was a conflict in heaven, the devil was warring with God. St. Michael and all his angels got together and threw the devil out of Heaven. He landed on earth - all that you can read in the Bible. But according to folklore he landed in a blackberry bush, hurt himself and swore revenge on St. Michael.

Every year since then he has avenged himself by piddling on all the blackberries on 29th September, which is why they taste so watery and should NEVER be eaten after Michaelmas!

What was eaten though was 'wayzgoose' - a goose that had been fattened on the corn stubbles. It was specially sacrificed to celebrate the season as commemorated in the saying 'The goose shall bleed on St. Michael's shrine'. It's meat made a tasty dish and its' grease was saved to rub on children's chests to keep away the ills and chills of winter - you remember? A goose was also given to the landlord with the half yearly payment of rent.

The 29th September was the day when pigs were allowed to roam the woods and rummage for food, acorns, beech mast and roots to fatten them up for killing at Martinmas (11th November). This right, given by most landowners, was called pannage. Cows and sheep could also graze any regrowth on the corn stubbles. For farmers and smallholders it was the time to start gathering bracken to bed their animals over the winter.

At Yarmouth, Michaelmas heralded the 'Herring Fair', where under the freedom of a Royal Charter anyone could sell fish for the next forty days. Especially welcome were Dutch fishermen for whom a special church service was held.

Shoals of red herrings were landed and sold. They were salted, smoked, dried and re-smoked until stiff, then sold inland to supplement winter rations and the meatless days of Lent. Even today Yarmouth is still famous for its smoked kippers and bloaters which are in fact Herrings!

The sacred woods of oak, yew and rowan were used on fires at this season.

In Scotland a lamb was sacrificed and eaten, also a 'St. Michael's Cake' containing a mixture of all the flours, wheat, oats, barley and rye, it had to be completely eaten during the day.

In London the 77 livery companies gathered to elect a new Lord Mayor and throughout the country magistrates were chosen. But in the countryside the question on everyone's lips was 'Are you staying on?' for farm workers were employed on an annual basis from Michaelmas to Michaelmas. It all began after the Black Death, when labourers were so scarce that every able bodied man had to offer himself for hire.

Magistrates fixed the wages for the coming year and announced them at the Michaelmas 'Statute of Labourers' sessions.

Farmers and workers assembled to hear what the terms were to be and most of the better workers were hired on the spot. The contract was sealed by the giving and acceptance of a 'fasten-penny' which could then be spent on food, drink and entertainment.

So began the 'Michaelmas Hiring Fair'. Those seeking work wore an emblem of their trade in their hat or on their smock, a leather whipcord knot for a carrier, a straw plait for the farm worker, a tuft of wool for the shepherd and piece of mop for a female servant which is why some were called 'mop fairs'.

For any person not satisfied with their new employer (or he with them) there was a way out - a 'Runaway Fair' was held on 11th November - Martinmas.

The reason for hiring staff at this time of the year was that it came at the end of the growing season, when hopefully the harvest had been successfully gathered in. Ploughing and preparations for next year's harvest were about to begin.

Michaelmas was the nearest religious festival to the Autumn Equinox. Farmers and landowners accepted the two Equinox dates for paying the half yearly rent, for transforming land and moving farms; which brings me nicely back to my opening paragraph - 'enough is enough'.

In the hymn 'Abide with Me' is a line 'change and decay in all around I see' - well, to be quite honest I never expected to live to see it, but for years it has been slowly creeping up on me, I have reached my 'sell by date'! My wife and I have joined the growing band of senior citizens who as a reward for the achievement of reaching the statutory age of retirement receive a weekly payment from the state, which seems to suggest that I'm in the preliminary throes of 'decay'. As for 'change' - there won't be that much money left over.

In farming I feel we are passing through an unnecessarily unsettling time. We no longer have a free hand over our future, 'quotas' limit our milk production, 'set-aside' reduces our corn crops by 15% even though much of the world is undernourished. There are endless, often irrelevant forms and the ever present spectre of VAT returns, to fill in by a certain date - or else!

From 1st October all animals will have to have new ear tags to comply with EEC regulations. On November 1st the 'Milk Marketing Board' which has served dairy farmers and consumers so well for over 60 years is to be replaced by private contracts with individual dairies or a new organisation to be known as 'Milk Marque'. Quite stiff penalties will be imposed on anyone not giving a years notice before ceasing milk production.

I still milk in an antiquated cowshed with 'bucket units' that 'went out with the ark' according to one salesman who unsuccessfully tried to sell me a new system. If I continue milk production those units and the metal work in my cowshed will have to be renewed at considerable expense. Another regulation states that in the future the dirty water from my cow, dairy and cowshed swillings will have to be kept separate from clean rainwater, stored in a tank and spread back onto the fields during certain months. The estimated cost of installing new drains and a tank is a conservative £10,000! Finally to get to any field on my farm my cows have to go onto an ever busier road, and to get to half my farm they have to cross a speedy section of the A34. To reach the other side takes two of us, one to try to control the traffic with a large red flag which many drivers choose to ignore, the other to drive the cows across. It is even worse trying to stop a stream of traffic, everyone tries to play at 'being the last one through'.

With all these matters in mind what would you do if you were in my shoes - they'd probably be big enough I take size 13! Well, we have decided rather reluctantly, 'enough is enough', to call it a day and give up milking the cows.

Which is where 'Michaelmas' comes in. Because I am a tenant and rent the land the estate has kindly consented to take 40 acres of my farm off my hands. My wife and I can remain in our picturesque old farmhouse - formerly the village inn - and we can retain a couple of small fields 'to keep my hand in' so to speak.

So after well over 40 years my routine will change. I will no longer be milking my cows twice every day. It will certainly seem strange at first but that is one 'change' I shall have to accept and after all it may help to slow down my rate of 'decay'! In fact in some ways I'm rather looking forward to my new life but I am certainly going to miss my old 'matrons of the meadows' - my 'Golden Cross' herd of Golden Guernsey cows.

161 September Old Age
'THE WEAR AND TEAR OF LIFE - SURVIVAL OF THE FITTEST'

The summer bedding plants were blooming at their best, the runner beans were still producing good pickings - then came the frost. One night of -4°C put a premature end to their production. They were 'nipped in the bud' so to speak, their useful life was finished, they were not able to reach maturity and die back naturally.

It started me thinking - yes I do sometimes! Very few things in life live out their full potential, most succumb in one way or another before their time is up.

Man is the only species of the animal kingdom that plans for old age, even though retirement is not necessarily a means of prolonging life.

Birds and animals, plants and trees do not receive a golden handshake for achieving their golden years. Most are worn out by wear and tear long before their time. Unlike ourselves wildlife cannot relax and take things easier, they must always be on top form and on their guard. Should they lose any of their faculties they are at risk. A damaged wing, a broken bone, impaired vision or hearing, all mean they cannot be as agile and alert, which is when predators will pounce and be able to catch them.

Even in the wild continuous stress will shorten their lifespan. A prolonged drought or spell of cold or wet weather will weaken the resolve of both plants and animals to pull through. Plants that are growing vigorously seldom suffer from problems, but any plant that is poorly is attacked by predators of the plant world, aphids, mildew and fungus. It is nature's way of weeding out the weaklings.

Birds need to preen themselves regularly to maintain their plumage. They put a fine coating of oil on their beak from the oil gland - the parson's nose - on top of their tail. They run it over every feather to make it water-proof.

If the bird becomes poorly its oil gland stops working. With water-birds the feathers become waterlogged, the bird sinks and drowns; whilst landbirds get wet through when it rains and having no insulation against the cold soon perish. This oiling of their feathers - preening - is the reasoning behind the old saying to run 'like water off a duck's back'.

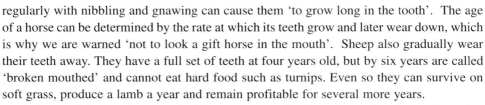

Rats, rabbits and mice have a problem with their teeth which if not worn down regularly with nibbling and gnawing can cause them 'to grow long in the tooth'. The age of a horse can be determined by the rate at which its teeth grow and later wear down, which is why we are warned 'not to look a gift horse in the mouth'. Sheep also gradually wear their teeth away. They have a full set of teeth at four years old, but by six years are called 'broken mouthed' and cannot eat hard food such as turnips. Even so they can survive on soft grass, produce a lamb a year and remain profitable for several more years.

It is a well known fact that the biggest enemy of a sheep is another sheep. Intensive stocking soon produces a build up of disease, the most common with overcrowded pastures is internal parasites, intestinal worms. These themselves may not kill a sheep but they will lower its resistance to other forms of attack.

The natural oil which a sheep produces to water-proof its fleece is called 'Lanolin'. Any setback may disrupt its production, the wool remains wet after rain and blow flies are attracted by the dampness or the clagged manure around the sheep's tail caused by diarrhoea as a result of worms.

The blow fly lays its eggs which turn into maggots that eat into the flesh, causing further distress and if not treated, ultimately death. That is one of the many reasons sheep are 'dipped' regularly.

ADULT LIVER FLUKE

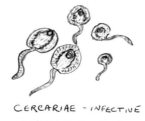

CERCARIAE - INFECTIVE
LARVAE LIVER FLUKE

Lots of sheep together can also spread footrot, the animal goes lame, loses condition and is more likely to be attacked by flies. Low lying meadows often have water snails which act as a host to another tiny worm which when mature climbs the damp stalks of grass. Sheep and young livestock grazing the leaves digest the worms which accumulate in the liver, honeycombing it with holes and if not treated, prove fatal. The worm is called 'liver fluke', we once lost a couple of calves with it.

A gradual build up of disease also affects birds which nest in the same place year after year such as swallows, blue tits and hawks. They build up a legacy of mites that suck the strength from the growing chicks and weaken them so much that many die. To help prevent it happening swallows nests should be knocked down and bird boxes thoroughly cleaned every year.

Too many birds or animals of the same type in an area may lead to a shortage of food, hence the reason that birds sing to mark their territorial feeding and breeding grounds. Animals mark their boundaries with faeces or squirt urine. Birds send their fledglings packing to find new feeding grounds whilst young shrews throw their parents out instead!

I often see an old rook strutting around the hedgerow followed a day or two later by a pile of feathers showing a fox has found it. Very few of my hens ever live to a ripe old age, here too the fox is usually responsible for their demise.

I often notice that if one of my cows was ostracised by the rest of the herd it wouldn't be long before some symptom would show up. The animals sensed it long before I ever did. This is the type of animal which in the wild would become the next meal for the jackal, lion or cheetah. They seldom chase an animal in prime condition. Their targets are the young, the old and the infirm.

It is, as the saying goes, 'the survival of the fittest' for 'Nature is red in tooth and claw'.

When I started farming we had a shorthorn cow that had a problem - an incurving horn.

If the end wasn't cut off regularly it would have grown into her head and killed her.

Against defects, deformities and diseases such as these nature has a remedy, they either don't breed or the young don't survive. In our civilised society we often lay up problems for ourselves by allowing and even encouraging those with defects to live as normal a life as possible.

This has come to the fore with the inbreeding of certain types of dogs who now suffer at an early age from inherent diseases. Another instance is in keeping the 'runt' of the litter, which seldom does as well as those born fit and healthy.

So far we have dealt mainly with animals and birds whose lives are shortened, but have you noticed trees whose branches are dying back especially from the crown, the furthest distance the sap has to travel from the roots. Very often the trunk is hollow and decayed, fungus is growing on the bark and toadstools on the ground where the roots have rotted. A gale and the tree comes crashing down, unable to stand the strain.

Beetles, woodlice and woodworm, mosses and fungi all start breaking down the cellulose so that it can be used by even smaller insects and bacteria as food. It's nature's way of cleaning up the countryside and returning the residual goodness to the ground to help other things to grow. It is an ever continuing cycle.

Just imagine what life would be like if people never passed on, if everyone and everything that had ever lived were still with us today. What a crowded world it would be. So whether we like it or not there is a lot to be said for the way that nature cleans everything up so neatly to make room for the next generation to follow along.

162 November Hibernation
'BEDDING DOWN FOR WINTER - SURVIVING THE ELEMENTS'

At this time of year when the days are short and dreary and the nights long and weary, do you sometimes wish that like 'Sleeping Beauty' you could quietly fall asleep, remain oblivious to the rigours of winter and be awakened by the kiss of the warm sun next spring? It is a dream many of us would like to share, to wake up on the further side of our problems, to find that they have solved themselves while we slumbered.

Unfortunately life is not that simple. We are not programmed to go into a period of suspended animation and hibernate through the difficult months of the year like some species.

In nature there are three ways to survive the winter: 1. Migrate, 2. Fatten-up and struggle through, 3. Hibernate.

The first solution, to migrate to a warmer and more hospitable climate is only done by a few; swallows, swifts, martins and cuckoos among them.

Their main reason for leaving our shore is answered by the age old question, 'Where do all the flies go in the wintertime?' If they stayed there wouldn't be enough food to keep them alive so of necessity they have to seek it elsewhere.

Our animals cannot migrate because we live on an island, they have to stick it out.

The second method of survival is to put on layers of fat during the months when food is plentiful and live off that, plus whatever can be scavenged during the 'hungry' months.

People formerly used this method. It is widely accepted that fat people do not feel the cold as much as those who are thin, fat acts as an insulating shield against the cold.

During the autumn and early winter folks feasted and fattened themselves so that their chances of surviving the lean months was far greater than anyone who remained thin. Our varied climate with its extremes of weather taxed the resources of even the hardiest, only those who were fat, fit and strong could compete, or so it was thought.

It became fashionable to be fat, those who were liberally endowed were usually the first to marry, whilst those who were skinny might not last until the spring so got left on the shelf.

With both animals and birds the trigger factors to make them start putting down reserves are twofold - decreasing daylight and a drop in temperatures.

They set in motion a complete system of linking rhythms that affect the eye, brain, pituitary and adrenal glands, producing hormones that retard development until the spring.

This does not happen if artificial light is used to replace daylight. Hens will continue laying in battery and deep litter units if provided with an everlasting summertime of artificial light.

In many species extra layers of hair, fur or feathers grow to increase their winter insulation. Our Shetland pony has a short thin coat in summer and a longer thick coat in winter.

Quite a few animals and birds also have temperature controls over various parts of their body to conserve energy. The heart and trunk remains warm but the extremities are many degrees cooler - my wife says my body must work on this system - when I crawl into bed half frozen!

As the length of daylight continues to shorten and the temperature fall, the butterfly caterpillar changes into a chrysalis and moth grubs retreat into a woven cocoon. Mature butterflies, especially the peacock, painted lady, small tortoiseshell as well as Queen wasps creep into crevices in hollow trees, folds in household curtains or hide behind pictures and mirrors.

Ladybirds gather in family clusters under tree bark or cracks in buildings, Snails congregate in holes or behind stones and seal the entrance to their shell with mucus which solidifies into a permeable epiphragm, a protective layer, like a porous eggshell.

Because insects and small mammals seem to just disappear it was originally thought that they died and were miraculously reborn in the spring. We know that frogs and toads find some soft mud to burrow beneath or alternatively they may seek a dry sheltered hollow beneath a covering of leaves. The sunken openings of our cellar windows are a favourite haunt, so much so that we always refer to them as the 'frog holes'.

Grass snakes, adders, slowworms and lizards find a safe refuge and retreat into a state of torpor to reduce their demand for food.

Worms are not active in severe weather, they curl up in deep caverns. This is unfortunate for the mole who has to eat his bodyweight of food every day to survive. To save up for a winters day he stores hundreds of worms in special 'larders'. To stop them escaping he punctures each one just below the head in such a way that it is paralysed but does not die. If the mole fails to return to feast upon them they gradually recover and can make good their escape.

Some fish such as chub, roach, dace, perch and minnows 'retire' into deeper water and become relatively inactive. In freezing weather smashing the ice may cause them to die of shock, a better method is to make a round hole with a hot water bottle then float a rubber ball to help stop it icing over again.

People once believed that because swallows darted just above the surface of ponds catching insects in the summer, they spent the winter months coagulated into a ball in the mud at the bottom. Cuckoos were thought to change into hawks and over-winter inside fairy hills.

In severe weather rabbits remain in their burrows and eat their soft faeces obtaining considerable further nutrients from their re-digestion, the resulting pellets are very hard and excellent for use in pea shooters!

During spells of bad weather the squirrel shelters in its drey in a lethargic state, only venturing out during warmer intervals to sniff out the scent of one of its many caches of stored nuts and acorns. It is estimated that up to 90% of small creatures die in a very hard winter.

The third way of combating the extremes of cold is called diapause in insects and hibernation in animals.

Probably because of our unstable climate we only have a few hibernants, hedgehogs, tortoises, bats and dormice. Urged on by instinct they fatten up and seek snug dry winter quarters, then through a chemical change these warm blooded mammals become cold blooded.

The pancreas pours extra insulin into the bloodstream, lowers the blood sugar, the magnesium increases, the body thermostat - the hypothalamus - at the base of the brain is turned down, the temperature reduces and the animal feels cold to the touch.

In this curled up half frozen state its digestion and pulse almost cease, it uses only one hundredth of its normal oxygen requirement and it enters into a condition scarcely distinguishable from death itself. This enables it to survive for months, blissfully unconscious of the cruel world outside.

However, there are drawbacks. A prolonged period of warm weather may wake the creature prematurely - a false spring. Quite a large amount of fat is used warming and waking into activity. Several warm spells can deplete the reserves so much that it dies.

Alternatively, extremes of cold cause the sleeper to use its body fat at a higher rate to maintain even its very low temperature - with fatal consequences. To help avoid these two extremes they insulate themselves inside a nest of leaves, grasses and mosses.

Especially before Christmas hedgehogs who are lighter sleepers will arouse and forage for food during warmer spells and bats occasionally make a brief winter appearance, then move deeper into their belfreys, roof cavities or caves and cling tightly huddled together like clumps of withered leather. Meanwhile the drowsy dormouse who starts its hibernation 'as fat as butter', sleeps on and on!

In spring bats only take fifteen minutes to warm themselves sufficiently to fly. Hedgehogs and dormice may take several hours before they can move freely, but all emerge emaciated and ravenously hungry.

It has been discovered that 'hibernants' have layers of brown fat which is far more efficient at storing energy than white fat. Most newborn animals and babies have layers of this between their shoulder blades to warm themselves until they learn to shiver. In animals and man it is lost as they grow older but mice who perpetually live in cold stores retain their brown fat, which is how they manage to survive in such low temperatures.

Of course nowadays with our well filled fridges and overflowing supermarket shelves there is not the need for us to put on layers of fat to see us through the winter, famine and starvation no longer pose a problem. Instead of burning up our internal layers of fat to keep us warm we rely on external fossil fuels to maintain us at a comfortable temperature.

If we do have to venture outside into the cold and chilling winds of reality we put on our thermal underwear and extra layers of clothing to compensate for the layers of fat we once carried.

During the winter we now enjoy the best of both worlds. We can remain active and take an interest in all that is going on around us without worrying about where the next meal is coming from.

The only problem that we have to face in order to live in this marvellous modern wonderland is to find the money to pay for it.

So perhaps hibernation is not such a bad idea after all!

163 December Squire
'JOBS, LAND, SCHOOLS, CHARITY ALL CAME FROM THE SQUIRE'

Nowadays there are so many demands for our money. Some like 'Children in Need' or Remembrance Sunday are voluntary contributions. Others are compulsory, such as Social Security and taxation which claim our cash to fund our hospitals, schools, forces and to assist those caught up in the trauma of unemployment or the tremors of old age.

Yet for over a thousand years we had a simple system operating in our countryside which kept the majority of people in work, fed and clothed as far as was humanly possible at that time, almost free of charge.

In Anglo-Saxon days the hub around which parish life revolved was the 'Thanes'. After the conquest of 1066 they were replaced by Norman 'Barons'. As they integrated into the community they became 'Lords of the manor' or 'squires'.

In those days children of noble birth were sent away to other baronial estates to be educated as damsels and pages. They had to serve at table and thereby learnt table manners, they were encouraged to play music, sing, dance and learn horsemanship. The boys - pages - were also instructed in the arts of archery, swordsmanship and wrestling.

At fourteen the page became an 'esquire' which technically meant a 'shield bearer' to a knight. On achieving this title the youth could expand his knowledge by joining the services and see some of the world or if studiously inclined, could go to university, travel and socialise.

They returned, full of their new-found fund of knowledge, and when they inherited the estate, they slowly tried to put their ideas into practice. Not all settled to this humble lifestyle, many longed to return to the more exciting life of the city.

One way they had of achieving this was because they owned an estate and paid taxes, they had a right to vote and were eligible for election into Parliament.

If successful in their new career they would become 'estates men', now known as 'statesmen', their standing in the realm - 'status' - comes from the same word.

Almost of necessity the squire had to be a leader for under his command he had a small army of men, women and children. The estate was virtually self supporting, almost all work was done within walking distance. Few of his subjects ever ventured outside its boundary except perhaps to the local market and the annual fair.

Although the squire could delegate some of his responsibilities to his senior servants, the bailiff, steward and clerk of the works, and in the hall to the chamberlain, housekeeper, head butler and cook, he had always to keep his finger on the pulse of the parish.

The estate had within itself an intricate infrastructure, tried and tested by years of experience, in which everyone in the parish was employed. Often generations of families continued in the same job, woodmen and sawyers, carpenters, bricklayers, plumbers and masons, coachmen, footmen and gardeners. And in the hall - maids and manservants.

The majority took an interest in their work, were proud of their achievements and providing they did a satisfactory job, were not late for work, and did not get drunk too often, they had a steady job for life.

If they fell ill or succumbed to old age they were not turned out, for there was nowhere for them to go. They were given some lighter job to keep them occupied. The squire's retainers were in fact retained indefinitely until they finally found a resting place from their labours - in the churchyard.

The squire knew that the best way to keep his workers happy was to give them an acre or two of land on which to keep some stock which they could worry about. Perhaps a cow to provide milk and butter and a calf annually to fatten up and sell or be used as a replacement. A cade (orphan) lamb in springtime for the children to cuddle and play with, a few hens to supply them with eggs and the occasional boiling fowl, some geese to graze the grass on the village green and the common land, and of course a sty at the bottom of the garden for the family pig. Fed on household scraps with an extra bit of corn and some acorns to fatten it up in the autumn, it would be the highlight of their Christmas dinner and of a great many meals afterwards.

These were the things the squire knew his workers enjoyed looking after and talking about in their spare time.

The estate did not exist solely to look after the squire and his family, but for the benefit of every member of the community in any way connected to it.

For instance, in the hall meals had to be cooked not only for the family but for all the staff, anything from 20 to 100 hungry mouths to feed. Each person was allowed a bread ration of one and a half loaves a day - which is why the lower servants were nicknamed 'loafers'.

At night the maids slept in the attic dormitories of the hall and the boys in the mews (hawk house) or in the lofts above the stables.

Between the squire and his workers there was a genuine bond, ladies curtsied and men touched their caps in respect as he passed and he raised his hand or had a kindly word in exchange. He knew them all by name, the ties between them were of friendship, it was a case of civility not servility.

Workmen and women knew that if they had a problem he would lend a sympathetic ear, their roof would be re-thatched, their pig sty repaired or their dispute with a neighbour settled in a considerate way, without any charge to them. To most he was a paternal figure, a kind of second father. True, he may have had a few vices, a bit of gambling, horse racing or a liking for the ladies - but then, who didn't?

His whims, fancies and eccentricities were put down to inbreeding or upbringing for that was just how his father and grandfather had behaved before him - it ran in the family. Nevertheless, he was a pillar of society that supported and chaired all the local societies, agricultural, horticultural, hospital, school, army reserves, police, prisons as well as political.

He was the master of the local foxhounds, their kennels were hard by and the hounds regularly met at the hall. Hunt balls and other functions kept the staff busy preparing for weeks before the event - and several days afterwards clearing up. The 'point-to-point' races were held in the park and the adjacent fields of 'Home Farm'.

One thing the squire could not abide was poaching, especially game birds which had cost him dearly to rear. Because he was also the local magistrate anyone hauled up before him on such a charge was severely reprimanded and if an employee, would be lucky to keep his job.

As a reward for feeding his pheasants and partridges, and not interfering with them, tenants and estate workers received a brace as a gift at Christmas, or were sometimes invited to take part in a special shoot.

As patron of the church the squire imposed it upon himself to set an example in religious matters. He had a special pew at the front of the church and before, during and after the service he would stand up and peer around to see which of his tenants or employees were missing. They had better have a good excuse ready when he next saw them or they would get a taste of his tongue.

When expensive repairs or alterations were wanted at the church, he was usually the first to contribute to start the fund rolling and frequently added another sizeable sum to complete the project. Land was also made available for a recreation ground, a village hall, a school or an extension to the churchyard, usually at a minimal rent for an eternal lease.

Bequests were often made in the squire's will for a weekly allocation of 'Dole bread' for the poor, or to provide a row of almshouses for the elderly.

It was an essential part of the church choir's Christmas routine to call at the hall at a set time to sing carols to the squire, his family, assembled guests and staff. Their dulcet tones were rewarded with a handsome donation to church funds, and more importantly to the younger members, platefuls of mince pies washed down with mulled wine served by the butler, who quietly reminded them to wipe their noses and not drop crumbs onto the polished floor.

Of course the other very important member of the hall was the squire's wife. Apart from bringing up the next generation she organised the staff in the hall and the cooking on a daily basis and was on hand to cope with any emergency during special events.

She made a special point of regularly visiting the sick, taking suitable gifts of fruit, vegetables or delicacies from the hall kitchen or garden as a treat. This was especially so at Christmas when in the days before Father Christmas distributed presents, the squire would accompany his wife on her rounds. They delivered hampers packed with items of food, clothing and good cheer as a token of gratitude to those who had served the estate so faithfully for the whole of their working life.

In the early days much of the money from the estate came from wool, which produced the 'wool barons'. Others gained in stature by amalgamating estates through astute marriages. Some expanded their fortunes during the Dissolution of the Monasteries.

In later times their wealth increased purely from profitable farming when certain squires became pioneers of stockbreeding and crop management, which led to higher returns. Most of this money was ploughed back into the estate for the benefit of the community.

Each squire in turn inherited the estate from his forbears and it was his duty to improve it and hand it to his heirs in course of time. It wasn't so much a case that the squire owned the land, it was rather that the land owned the squire.

The decline of the estates started with the Industrial Revolution, the higher wages paid in towns tempted workers away from the countryside. This coupled with higher taxation and the imposition of death duties, caused the break-up and sale of most of our country estates.

The few that still function are but a shadow of their former size and importance. In his way and in his day the squire served his country and his community to the best of his ability. Now, the 'State' funded by taxation has taken over the responsibilities of health, housing, employment and security that were formerly fulfiled almost single-handedly by the squire and his family practically free of charge, and furthermore he held the community together.

A very happy Christmas to you all.

164 January Winter Weather
'A YEAR'S WORTH OF WEATHER IN A WEEK'

An ancient saying states that a record of what happens during the first twelve days of January, will represent the months of the coming year. Another says that the feast of St Hilary, January 13th, is often the coldest day of the year.

Whether there is any truth in these sayings or not, within the first few days of this year we have already had almost every kind of weather, sunshine and showers, thunder and hail, rain and sleet, fog and frost, rime and snow. Even now the crisp snow crackles underfoot, its partially thawed surface has re-frozen into a glazed layer and looks just like the icing on a gigantic Christmas cake.

Yet in spite of the severity of the frost as I sit at my desk writing this and look out over the snow-covered lawn a dozen or so gnats are dancing up and down in the warmth of a shaft of sunshine that filters through the pine trees.

What causes our wintry weather, how does it all happen? Well, firstly because our world spins at a slight angle, 23 degrees, here in the Northern hemisphere our total daylight is only eight hours in mid-winter compared with eighteen hours in midsummer.

In addition the small amount of sunshine we do receive is beamed in at an angle reducing its earth warming power. Also the further from the equator the cooler it becomes. Northern Scotland is on average six degrees cooler than southern England. Another factor is the height above sea level, as air rises it gets thinner and is cooled by expansion, approximately 3°C for every thousand feet.

It is said that we do not have a climate, just changes of weather, so how is our weather formed? Our wobbly world is surrounded by a gaseous mixture which we call atmosphere. It consists of about 78% nitrogen and 21% oxygen, the remainder includes carbon dioxide and water vapour and is not perfectly transparent. Just as a thin garment hides a figure from prying eyes so our atmosphere shields us from the penetrating glare of solar heat and ultra-violet rays.

The water vapour that exists in the air has been exhaled by plants or has evaporated from the earth. At a certain temperature, the air becomes so saturated with water vapour that it changes into a liquid state - this is called the 'dew point'. Billions of these minuscule condensed water droplets or ice crystals crammed close together become what we call 'clouds'.

It takes about two thousand of these tiny droplets to make one raindrop. It will eventually fall to earth with a maximum speed of 18 mph. However there are often winds or warmer air currents that surge upwards faster than that. They lift the tiny raindrops many thousands of feet, super cooling them on the way. Some collide with ice crystals and transform into miniature ice pellets, and eventually they start falling. On their way down they collide with rising liquid droplets which freeze onto their surface giving them a further coating of ice. This cycle can be repeated twenty five or more times, sometimes lifting the ice pellets to a height of seven miles at a speed of up to fifty mph before they finally fall as hailstones.

Their size varies according to the number of coatings of ice, from quite common pea grains through the leaf stripping, glass breaking, 'golf balls', to the largest on record, two pounders of grapefruit size which devastated parts of Kansas, USA in 1970.

Hail falls from Cumulo Nimbus 'storm' clouds hence hailstorms. The thunder which frequently accompanies it is caused by the friction between the masses of rising (positive) and falling (negative) water droplets or ice crystals. They create a positive electrical charge at the top of the storm cloud and a negative charge at the bottom. When they build a sufficient charge of several million volts a current of many thousand amps flashes between them and neutralises the static, we call it 'sheet lightning'. If the negatively charged bottom of the cloud discharges to the positive earth beneath it causes 'forked lightning'.

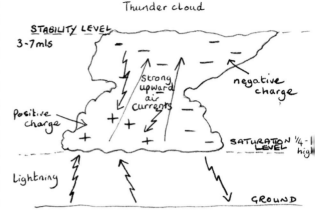

Its track to earth is only about two inches in diameter. It heats the surrounding air to an amazing thirty thousand degrees centigrade, expanding it at supersonic speed with an explosive force of up to a hundred times normal air pressure. This shock wave becomes the sound wave which we call 'thunder'. The difference in the speed of light at 186,000 miles per second and the speed of sound at 760 miles per hour means that every five seconds counted between the lightning flash and the thunder represents a distance of a mile. The echoing rumbles that follow the first crack come from the varying distance of its twenty miles of torturous twisting paths.

People feared storms at this season for they forecast 'winter thunder, winter thunder, poor man's death and rich man's hunger'. They also fulfiled another saying - 'what the summer gets, the winter eats,' for storms meant that more food was needed to feed the wintering stock. The name given to a 'wind' is the direction from which it blows, thus 'the 'North Wind' doth blow and we shall have snow'.

When it snowed my mother used to tell me it was 'the old woman in the sky, plucking her geese,' the white snowflakes were their feathers. I would press my nose against the window pane and peer upwards trying to catch a glimpse of her! 'Snow' is formed by the crystallisation of thousands of tiny water droplets at temperatures below freezing. If wet they collide with one another and stick together forming the kind of snowflakes that make good snowballs. The largest flakes on record fell in Siberia in 1971 and measured fourteen inches diameter, far bigger than dinner plates.

Although of different thickness, snow crystals are always six sided and such are the myriad variation and combinations of the pattern that it is widely believed that of all the snow that has ever fallen upon earth no two snowflakes have ever been the same. That's absolutely incredible isn't it.

Another interesting fact is that because the snow at the poles never melts it has been there since the dawn of time, scientists can drill down, take samples and calculate when contamination from natural catastrophes such as volcanic eruptions occurred many, many thousands of years ago.

Incidentally returning to the wind, when it rotates clockwise (i.e. from North to East) it 'veers' and if it rotates anticlockwise (i.e. from East to North) it 'backs'.

With the warmth from even the weakest winter sunshine the temperature rises slightly.

If there is a layer of cloud at night it acts as an insulating barrier and stops the residual heat escaping into the upper atmosphere. In other words the clouds act like a blanket, keeping the earth beneath warmer, which is why it is called a 'blanket of cloud'.

If there is no cloud heat escapes and we are likely to have a cold frosty night when the stars shine as though they have been polished. People who behave in a 'cold' way to others are often termed 'frosty', whereas those who 'shine' frequently become 'stars'.

As the earth cools at night the water vapour immediately above it becomes saturated and condenses into tiny droplets - the previously mentioned 'dew point'. These miniscule droplets settle onto any cooler surface such as cobwebs, grass, leaves and twigs in a form that we call 'dew'.

Which reminds me of the country yokel walking to work at dawn who met a buxom young maiden. 'Some dew,' he exclaimed cheerfully, - 'and some don't' she replied frostily. Which leads me on to say that if the temperature is below freezing when the dew forms it becomes a 'rime' or 'hoar frost'. Then the dew transforms everything it touches into a fragile white lace-like beauty so beloved by amateur photographers. Should the super cooled dew droplets land on a windowpane they produce the picturesque leafy 'fern' patterns as they freeze.

'Dew point' is also responsible for another feature of windless winter days, 'fog' - when visibility falls below two hundred yards; above that it is called 'mist'.

'Fog' is in fact 'cloud' at ground level. It is particularly dangerous when it forms in patches, perhaps above a river, or as a result of cold air rolling downwards into a valley.

Even deadlier is when super cooled dew or ice cold rain falls onto frozen ground, creating the almost invisible, treacherous surface known as 'glazed' or 'black' ice, which, because it is so smooth has very little friction and is the cause of many accidents. It can also be deadly to perching birds, it freezes their feet to the branches, they are held prisoner, shackled with ice until it thaws.

Frost also causes other serious setbacks. Birds have to bathe to clean and preen their feathers even in wintertime. Prolonged frost freezes puddles, pools, pits and ponds, feathers become greasy and clogged, their insulation is less efficient, the bird suffers, or may even die as a result.

The natural camouflage of birds and mammals is useless against a background of snow. They are easily spotted by their predators. On the other hand mice, voles and shrews can lead lives that are largely unobserved underneath a canopy of decaying bracken, or under a protective coverlet of snow that keeps everything underneath insulated from the freezing conditions above.

An excessive weight of snow can break the branches of conifers and several frosts can blacken the buds of broadleaved trees so that the leaves do not open in the spring.

Yet underneath them the snowdrops are already speckling the ground with their white blossom. They hang their heads so that the rain does not wash the drop of succulent nectar from their fairy lanterns. In very severe weather they transfer their sap into vacant air cells so that when it freezes it does not damage the living tissue.

When it thaws they lay dehydrated for an hour or two until the sap melts and returns to its proper cells then the stems and leaves stand upright once more.

Darkness has fallen. As I look out of my window I see the first sliver of the new moon - lying on its back - holding water in its lap, a sure sign of bad weather to come?

These first days of January have exactly fitted the description of winter that I learnt as a child from one of my dad's old farmhands 'first it blew and then it snew, and then it friz and then it thew, and arter that it rained'. I wonder if the next twelve months will follow that same pattern?

165 February False Teeth
'CHEWING OVER THEIR HISTORY'

At least, here is a subject that you can really get your teeth into, for although they are used by over half our population every day of the week, they seldom come out in conversation.

When I was a lad an elderly lady came to help my mother each wash day. As she sat down to dinner she would discreetly remove her false teeth and hide them under the tablecloth. After dinner she slipped them back in, and I was fascinated by them. They reminded me of the old Music Hall joke, 'Your teeth are like the stars, they always come out at night'.

Until quite recently teeth were more likely to be considered a cosmetic addition to vanity than an aid to the digestion of food. After all, the smile of a pretty girl would not look anything like as attractive if it shone from a toothless face, would it? A simple proof of this is how easily a facial poster can be disfigured by blacking one or more of the front teeth.

Indeed the reason why portraits of our monarchs looks so stern, seldom smiling or showing their teeth is most probably that they hadn't any. It is said that Queen Elizabeth I inserted pads to hide her rotten stumps and hollow cheeks whenever she appeared in public or posed for her portrait.

The intense pain of severe toothache was certainly a considerable factor in many of the foul tempers and bad judgements made by the leaders of yesteryear. Even so the discomfort of toothache or 'distemper' as it was then called, was considered less painful than the torture of having them pulled out.

In the countryside teeth were removed by anyone with a strong enough arm and the tools for the job, blacksmiths and cobblers being the most usual, followed by school teachers only a class or so behind.

At fairs, 'quack' doctors and charlatans claimed to remove them painlessly. The screams of the sufferers were drowned by the banging of drums and blowing of horns, an accompaniment that drew even larger crowds and more 'patients' egged on by their friends, who took sadistic delight in seeing others suffer.

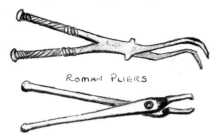

Roman Pliers

Dentists - 'barber' surgeons of 1300-1745 advised withdrawing bad teeth slowly, thus prolonging the agony. 'Quacks' ripped them out quickly, lessening the duration of the immediate pain but frequently they broke or dislocated the victim's jaw or severed a nerve in doing so.

Bad teeth were blamed for many illnesses of the blood, they had to come out. Toothless gums soon hardened sufficiently to eat 'soft' foods, meats were minced as lumps could not be chewed, hence 'mince-pies'. Many people carried 'masticators' - like large nut crackers, for crushing their food.

Unfortunately a complete loss of teeth, coupled with shrinkage of the gums often led to the over-closing of the lower jaw which caused premature deafness. It also gave people a haggard look, where the nose curved down and the chin curved up - still widely featured in cartoonists caricatures of ugly old women, hags and witches.

From Greek and Roman times onwards the rich were fitted with individual teeth of gold - a sure sign of their affluence. They were initially held in place with gold wire or silk thread and fastened on to adjacent healthy teeth, but as they were seldom cleaned and never removed they soon gained a firm coating of tartar which frequently caused diseased gums and bad breath. The need to mask their bad breath and deflect the obnoxious odour was one of the main reasons for ladies of fashion to flirt behind their fans from 1550s to the 1900s.

Many used mouth washes and tooth cleaners of annis-seed, burnt alum, mint and cloves in a solution of lemon juice, vinegar, wine or honey rubbed on with a sponge or cloth covered finger, but as there were no toothbrushes they had little effect. Diluted nitric acid or an abrasive pumice powder certainly whitened teeth but soon wore away the enamel as did grit in the food, causing cavities through which bacteria could enter and cause decay.

Prayers and incantations were said, and amulets and talismen worn as a prevention against, or remedy for the toothache which inevitably followed.

Of course there were many attempts at filling cavities. A widespread practice among the poor was to insert slivers of sealing wax into the hole and melt it with the point of a red hot nail. The rich used molten lead, gutta-percha or gold foil applied by layer and pummelled in place and from about 1830 the extremely dangerous combination of mercury and silver. During both extractions and fillings patients were often immobilised by being fastened to the dentist's chair with leather straps, or held down on the floor by relations and friends, or burly men hired specifically for the job.

Because sound teeth symbolised youth and vigour, and the loss of them weakness and old age, vanity decreed that no avenue of introducing false teeth into the mouth to make a person appear young should remain unexplored.

Apart from fashioning artificial teeth from gold, teeth were taken from whales, sheep and dogs. The most popular and effective were made from ivory, carved from elephant or walrus tusks, and although they had the drawback of being darkened by Port wine they were used almost up to this century.

'Natural' (human) teeth were bought by the bucketful. 'Resurrectionists' removed them from the mouths of the recent deceased before selling the corpses for dissection to medical schools. Gangs of tooth drawers followed armies into battle and extracted teeth from the dead and dying. They were known as 'Waterloo teeth'. Later teeth were shipped by the barrel from the fallen of the American Civil War. Sometimes they were boiled or cleaned before insertion, but more often not.

The most satisfactory results came from fresh teeth in a system that was regarded as 'Robbing Peter to pay Paul'. Poor country folk would have a sound tooth removed, it was immediately inserted into the socket left by an extracted decayed one of a wealthy person. The Yokel would gain some immediate spending money and providing the transplant took, the rich might obtain several years use from it.

This method overcame the replacement of individual teeth but if a whole mouthful were required it took six weeks for a skilled craftsman to rivet a full set of human teeth onto an ivory plate. The base then had to be carved away a fraction at a time to try to make a reasonable fit, which it seldom did.

The trouble with nearly all early dentures was that they permanently covered up the rotting stumps underneath. One comment was that they were 'Mausoleums of gold over a mass of sepsis'. Everything eaten became contaminated often causing stomach and other infections.

A partial success came around the 1800s when Josiah Wedgwood from the Potteries started moulding sets of teeth in porcelain, pipe clay and earthenware. Thousands were produced. They had several advantages. They could be removed and cleaned, they were hardwearing and they didn't discolour or decay.

The disadvantages were that they were 'hard' to wear, brittle in use, inclined to be unnaturally white and they grated. With the customary bad fitting they 'clicked' whenever the wearer breathed or talked. But they could be ordered through the post! The only fitting possible was to try them, if they were wearable they were usable. 'The inconvenience of the first few days is only transient', it was said.

If only the bottom set was required lead weights were inserted to help to hold it in place. To stop the upper set falling down coiled gold springs were inserted at the rear of the full sets. These had the effect of forcing the jaw apart and wearers walked and worked open mouthed as a result. Because of the lack of individual fitting they would easily slip and protrude like the teeth of a neighing horse.

Another danger was when the wearer sneezed the force of air would expel the teeth onto the floor, the fire or into the food. Even worse was being caught by a bout of sea sickness, many a set has finished up on the floor of the ocean, leaving the owner even more at sea than before.

Wealthy patients who wanted their teeth fitted were visited in their homes by the dentist. In order to ensure their continued custom he always removed the front teeth first even if they were still sound, since no one wished to be without the essential visible front teeth.

During this often prolonged period of extraction, waiting six months for the gums to shrink and harden, then moulding, making and fitting the new dentures, Victorian ladies would temporarily withdraw from society. They would take their meals in their rooms so that they would not be seen in such a shameful condition by others.

Because handmade sets of teeth were so expensive they were often passed on to another recipient on the death of the owner. My mother used to tell the tale of a posh lady who turned up at a dinner then found she had forgotten to put her teeth in. However the elderly gentleman she sat next to put his hand into his pocket and produced a pair. Unfortunately they were too big. He shuffled around in another pocket and produced another pair which fitted perfectly. 'My word he is a good dentist' she later said to her host, to which he replied, 'He's not a dentist he's our local undertaker.'

If the roots of the individual teeth were still sound the porcelain crown could be attached with a wooden peg. The peg would swell with moisture from the saliva and hold the crown in place. Sometimes it swelled too much and shattered the crown or splintered the root.

A FEW EXTRACTS FROM THE HISTORY OF DENTISTRY:
 * The first patent for a suction plate was granted to a Connecticut confectioner in 1848
 * Two years later 'Vulcanite', a sulphur hardened rubber was introduced.
 * An American dentist watched a stage performance where a 'patient' was given a whiff of Nitrous Oxide, felt no pain and woke up laughing - the idea of the anaesthetic laughing gas was born.
 * A satisfactory tooth cement came into being about the same time, and the dreaded dentist's drill, around the 1870s.
 * It wasn't until the 1920s that only properly trained dentists were allowed to practice.
   I suppose that up until then they had only been practising.

But what still strikes me as strange is that, even today, with all our advances in technology, my teeth will ache for ages, but the pain will miraculously cease just before the time for my appointment at the dentist's surgery.

166 March Parish Priests
'.....WHO HAVE SERVED THROUGH THE AGES'

In bygone days employment and the social life of the village revolved around the squire, but its spiritual life was centred on the Church. A great deal has been written about the architecture and importance of ecclesiastical buildings, yet very little is known about the priests who served them throughout the ages.

About fifteen hundred years ago a new concept of worship 'Christianity' began to spread around our island. Its message was carried by monks who wandered far and wide teaching and preaching to the country 'heath dwellers' - 'heathen' people - about a loving God, then converting them to this new religion.

Unfortunately their visits were few and far between, people soon slipped back to worshipping their former gods. To overcome this obstacle a few recently converted and enthusiastic leaders of the Anglo-Saxon Thanes built small wooden churches and installed chaplains to satisfy the spiritual needs of themselves, their families and their workers.

The Thane also provided a parcel of land to support both the church and the chaplain in future. As he paid all the costs the Thane held the 'Right of Presentation', in other words he and his heirs became the patrons of the living and could appoint a Priest of their choice, usually with the additional agreement of the Abbot or Bishop. A system which has continued, where the 'squire' has survived, until today.

The Priest held the position of a senior servant in the household and either lived in the hall or was provided with a 'parsonage' house. He was allocated twice the number of strips of land of a commoner, to cultivate for his daily bread. The villagers paid him a 'Scot', a tax of one penny a hearth and one penny a plough and presented him with the Easter offering, a custom that has continued until recently in many churches.

When a person died the Priest received a 'soul scot', initially the second best animal the deceased owned - the squire claimed the best. Later it was called a 'heriot' and was paid in cash.

Another source of income came from the tithe, one tenth of the year's production of the parish, of which the Priest was allowed one third, the church and the poor shared the rest. Originally this was a voluntary contribution, but after 990 AD tithes became a compulsory tax and a constant cause of consternation. The Priest's 'parish' varied in size from a few acres to several square miles often covering several manors and so vast that in order to know where his ministry began and ended all the parishioners joined him once a year to 'beat the bounds'. At each marking point on the boundary youngsters were beaten (with willow wands) on their bottoms to impress the position of the landmarks on their memory.

As the parochial system matured, forests were cleared, new manors were made and fresh parishes formed. But in this era of expansion corruption began to set in. Patrons appointed monks as Priests. They were not used to pastoral work and the hard graft of farming, so they obtained a chaplain to do the work for them. The monk still demanded his full share of the tithe, paid the chaplain a small allowance and kept the rest for himself, only the honest ones gave the extra back to the Patron or their monastery.

Each Priest was originally to have the 'cure of souls' or 'curacy' of only one parish where he was termed a 'Rector' (ruler). He received the major tithes from ploughed ground of corn, hay and wool and a wage of fifty marks a year. Of lesser importance was the 'Vicar' who deputised and did his duties for him. He received only the tithes from spade dug ground, orchards and gardens plus about five marks.

Like the monks, rectors would appoint vicars to do their work and pocket the surplus cash for themselves. Some became very greedy, they bought up vacant rectorships, appointed vicars and never preached or even entered the church for which they officially held the living.

The hard pressed, penniless vicars often had to serve several parishes in order to obtain a living wage, others took on additional work, many even became innkeepers especially in Wales.

Although Rectors were generally well-educated, vicars were often novices, few had much knowledge of the Bible, and sermons were only given about four times a year.

Most of the services were supposed to be in Latin, the congregation couldn't understand them and with the corruption and lowering standards many of the chaplains couldn't either. Those who could read and write were called 'clerk' from which we derive 'Cleric', 'Clergyman' and 'Clerk in Holy Orders'.

In early Norman times there were only 900 registered Priests but there were 4000 other ordained men, deacons, assistants, curates, exorcists, clerks, chantries, doorkeepers and readers. One in three of the male population was registered in one way or another with a monastery or church.

The minimum age for a Priest was set at twenty four, and the majority stayed in one Parish, serving until they dropped, many gave up to sixty years devoted service. The honourable and honest ones toiled hard and far outweighed the lazy and dishonest incumbents.

Rich livings were, as a rule, the result of having a Parish on very fertile ground yielding an abundance of tithes. Poor livings came from sandy, swampy, heathland or heather farming where yields were small.

The Black Death (c1350) drastically reduced the number of clergy. Minor ordinands were promoted by Bishops who never inquired too closely into their qualifications as long as the vacancy could be filled.

Much of the Priests' time was taken up working on their own strips of land, managing the Glebe land which had been

given to the church and dealing with flocks of sheep and hives of bees all donated by generous benefactors who had 'passed on' with the plague.

Because of the pressure of work Priests were so busy that they said their canonical hours in the fields to avoid wasting time returning to church. They provided their own robes, some couldn't afford a new set so they wore the same ones all their life.

Even fewer clergy were now sufficiently educated to be able to preach. If they could read they delivered a service, if not they made it up as they went along. There was no uniformity either of services or between churches until after the reformation (1535).

Travelling friars still gave most of the sermons in church. They roused the congregation with their verbal threats of 'hell, fire and brimstone' torment in the next life, as depicted in the 'last judgement' paintings on church walls.

The monks message was 'Prepare yourselves for happiness in the next world by being miserable in this'. Their intrusion was not welcomed by the less articulate, humble, penniless, parish priest who preached on local misdemeanours, used humour and told stories to get his message across in his own Chantry Chapel or Chapel of Ease. The main Churches were known as Mother churches and it was at these that most of the baptisms, marriages and burials had to take place, denying the local pastor of this increase to his 'stipend', as his salary was called.

However large or small the church it was a place of splendour to the parishioners who lived in squalor, but to the parson the taking of services had many complications when compared with the present day. There were no seats, the congregation wandered around and chattered with one another, he had to raise his voice if he was to be heard above the clamour. The elderly and disabled leant against the columns or walls for support, hence the expression 'the weakest to the wall'. Others sat or squatted on the foul rushes on the floor in the company of the many dogs who wandered in and out at will. When it was time for his flock to receive the mass, the Priest would warn them by ringing a special 'Sanctus Bell'.

In spite of what we would now term turmoil, local people took great pride in their churches and their ministers which led to considerable rivalry between parishes. To help enforce discipline and oversee any abuses, 'Synodsmen', or 'Sidesmen' as they soon came to be called, were appointed to aid him. The Priest selected two of them to act in a much closer capacity, they were known as Church Wardens. Some of the parishioners became suspicious of this authority. It was resolved by one warden being chosen by the Priest, the other by the people. The main stumbling block in their duties was sorting out the complicated payment of tithe, a burden which was slowly being simplified by payment in cash instead of in kind.

In the early days of the church Priests were allowed to marry but later the rules were changed and like Monks they were supposed to remain celibate. This ruling was increasingly disobeyed. Some Priests employed 'housekeepers' known as 'concubines' to look after their needs and to bear their children. These ladies, 'conciliates', were excommunicated, they were not allowed to attend Mass and had to be buried on the North side of the churchyard. The strange quirk was that many of their children followed their fathers into the priesthood, some even rising through the ranks to become Bishops.

However the greatest period of religious change was soon to be put into motion by a Monarch who was no particular moralist himself, Henry VIII. He decided to abolish the authority of the Pope and the catholic church, with decisions enforced from Rome, and replace it with a Protestant Church in England having the sovereign at the helm.

167 April Religious Turmoil
'RELIGION, THE TARGET IN TIMES OF CHANGE'

For well over a hundred years before the Reformation there had been a growing groundswell of agitation among the clergy of both this and other European countries

They were questioning the wisdom of the supreme authority of the Church being in the hands of the Pope; the accumulating and often ill-gotten wealth of the monasteries; and the immoral practice of priests selling 'indulgences' - the promise of forgiveness of sins - then pocketing the money for themselves.

In England Ecclesiastics also wished to join the wave of new learning, the 'Renaissance', which had suddenly accelerated after the introduction of the printing press. They wanted their Latin Bible to be published in English so that it could be understood by everyone.

For the first 25 years of his reign Henry VIII disregarded their protests and was rewarded when the Pope honoured him with the title of 'Defender of the Faith'.

However, following his failure to obtain permission for divorce proceedings, the King utilised the groundswell of discontent to declare that England should become a Protestant country with himself as head of the Church. So was born the Church of England.

The Monasteries were broken up and their wealth passed to the 'Crown'. About ten thousand monks, nuns and friars were made redundant, some accepting the teachings of the new Church to become clergy. Most eventually found alternative work, the remainder begged for a living.

Any staunch Catholics who resisted the alterations were ruthlessly swept aside. A Bible in English was put into every church, and so great was the desire for learning that they had to be chained to prevent them being taken away to be read. The minor orders of the ordained, clerks, acolytes, sacristans, etc were disbanded.

There was a great striving to obtain educated men for the ministry. One serious drawback was that marriage was still forbidden. King Henry said 'Priests would breed too quickly!'.

That was roughly where the religious reforms of the reformation ended. Things remained reasonably calm for the clergy under their next ruler, the nine-year-old boy king, Edward VI, who issued a Protestant Prayer Book in English.

When he died seven years later his half sister Mary came to the throne. There was a drastic change. During her five year reign, she re-introduced Catholicism, had Protestant leaders burnt at the stake, and drove more than a thousand clergy from their churches. She lost the French wars, emptied the Exchequer, ruined the fleet, and on her death left England at a very low ebb.

She was followed by the 25-year-old Protestant Queen Elizabeth who, for the next 30 years, had to contend the throne against her younger rival, the Catholic widow, Mary Queen of Scots who had been married to the Dauphin of France for two years until he died.

In just 25 years religion in England had swung from Catholic to Protestant back to Catholic and now, under Elizabeth, to Protestant again. It's little wonder there were so few applicants for ordination. But by shrewd moves, Elizabeth began to change the fortunes of the Church and its ministers.

A new Ecclesiastic Court was set up - churchgoing became compulsory and was enforced by law. Catholics would not be punished for their faith but could not hold office in Church, ministers did not have to remain celibate, they could marry if they wished - as under Edward VI, then revoked by Queen Mary - though it did not become official for another 40 years.

This put an end to what, for a long time, had been a recognised 'sport' in many parishes, trying to lead the clergy 'astray' then reporting his misconduct to the Bishop. Rather than breaking his vows and having a mistress bear his children it was thought that marriage would provide a steadying influence.

It took a long time for parishioners to accept this state of affairs, mainly because the clergy did (as Henry VIII had predicted) raise large families who secured the best jobs for their offspring. A saying soon circulated was that 'England was never merry after priests were allowed to marry', but within a century the old prejudices had died away and the parson's wife was an indispensable part of village life.

By the end of Elizabeth's very successful 45-year reign there were much higher standards both in the church and among the clergy. Better educated sons from rich families were entering the ministry, but fewer clerics came from trades or humble backgrounds. The majority were now respected leaders within their spiritual realm.

But the pendulum was set to swing again. The death of 'Good Queen Bess' as she was affectionately called, marked the end of the Tudors (1603). The first Stuart King, James VI of Scotland, the son of Mary Queen of Scots, became James I of England thus uniting our two countries.

His greatest achievement was the publishing of the new translation of the Bible in 1611, still in current use in most of our churches. His great failing was to claim he ruled by 'Divine Right' and was above the law of the land and of Parliament.

He started enforcing his own rules and regulations and became very unpopular, especially when both the Roman Catholics and the extremist Protestants - the Puritans - were threatened with severe punishment if they refused to acknowledge the King as head of the Church. This led to Catholic disturbances still remembered on Guy Fawkes night and the departure of many extremist Puritans, 'Pilgrim Fathers', sailing first to Holland and then to America, rather than give up their religious beliefs.

Those that remained demanded two sermons a day, not two a year as had previously been the case. They refused to pay the stipends of the clergymen who held different views from their own, often openly putting forth their objections in church. The result was that many priests feared their parishioners more than their Bishop and left. The vacancies were bought up by the Puritans who installed their own people in them, often at more than three times the wage of previous curates. As a result open hostility arose between Anglicans and Puritans. Other bones of contention were that Puritans didn't wear the surplice when ordained, allow the wedding ring in marriage or give the sign of the cross at baptism. They refused to say the Lord's Prayer or use the prayer book but insisted on their own Geneva version.

Things reached a climax when Charles I became King and continued his fathers stance of ruling by 'Divine Right' and being above the law of the land, all of which resulted in the outbreak of Civil War in the 1640s. The Puritans rose to power, eventually under the leadership of Oliver Cromwell. The King was beheaded, 2500 Protestant clergy were dispossessed. Sports and games, bells, church fairs, holidays and Christmas festivities were banned. Stained glass windows were broken, rood screens shattered, churches were whitewashed covering the colourful paintings.

For the next twenty years religion was separated from the customs of the countryside. People were not allowed to enjoy themselves. When Oliver Cromwell was overthrown and the monarchy in the form of the Protestant Charles II restored, many of the quaint country customs, subdued by 20 years of abolition, never revived. Nearly two thousand Puritan clergymen were removed from office, but there was such a shortage of clergy that they were allowed to become ministers again providing they accepted the doctrine of the Church of England and moved at least five miles from their previous parish.

During the Civil War Royalists had worn their hair long. Puritans shaved or short cropped their hair which is why they were called 'Roundheads'. In order to try to hide their earlier leanings Puritan priests took to wearing wigs until their hair grew long. The trials and tribulations of the clergy throughout this stormy period are well recorded in the popular song 'The Vicar of Bray'.

The piety of the Puritans was largely responsible for the laxity in the laity that followed - the pendulum swings again. A parsonage post was very useful for installing the younger son of the local squire, or the squire's daughter could marry the curate. As the squire was the Patron of the living this was easy to arrange when a vacancy arose.

Respect was always shown to the Squire because he was the main employer but little reverence was shown to their offspring, the clergy, during divine worship. His status in society was more likely to be decided by how good a huntsman, sportsman or socialiser he was rather then any religious references. Money mattered - marry an heiress!

It was an affluent time for the richer clergy - good food, good wine and over indulgences. They wanted ever larger vicarages or rambling rectories with lots of staff to enhance their reputation, buildings which have become 'white elephants' of recent years.

The decline in the morals of the priests, especially towards the poor, led to the rapid rise of Methodism, first within the Church, then as a separate religion having their own churches, ministers and lay preachers. They had happy services full of hope with rousing hymns and stirring sermons. Ranters or not they drew the congregations away from the staid churches.

But at the other end of the clerical scale there were still very many hard-working, honest clergy, who, along with their wives, milked, raised pigs and poultry and a family as well as seeing to all the affairs of religion in the church and parish:

'Toes out of shoes, heels out of stockings, threadbare cassock in tatters. He had to preach to a church full of those on whom he was dependant for his financial assistance. He had to tread carefully, he dare not upset them, or he would be dismissed by his Patron, seldom, if ever, by his Bishop,' so a report stated.

However, some help was at hand, his wages were raised by the benevolence of Queen Anne's Bounty, when some £60,000,000 of Ecclesiastical dues that had been held by the Crown since the Dissolution of the Monasteries , was given back to the Church.

Even so he had two or more parishes to serve and walk between every Sunday, or for funerals during the week. A round trip of often ten miles or more. He and his wife ran the school, succoured the sick, aided the elderly and won the admiration and respect of the parishioners by sheer hard work and honest living.

The minister lived most of his life in the parish, had baptised, married and buried generations and was eventually laid to rest by those whom he had served so faithfully.

Looking back, the best parsons have not always been the most flamboyant or those that hit the headlines but those who were straightforward, honest, reliable and devoted to serving God and their fellow men to the best of their ability.

And finally, just to put preaching into perspective I read once that 'The message of the Church borne across the meadow by bells often has more impact than many a sermon preached over peoples' heads, or the melancholic melodies of the choirs of our great cathedrals.' It puts me in my place!

168 May Old Farm Tools
'WARTIME METHODS ON THE FARM - TOOLS FROM BYGONE DAYS'

A young farmer from another village asked me last week, 'Do you happen to have any old farm tools that would have been in use during the last war that we could borrow for our county showground display to commemorate the fiftieth anniversary of Victory in Europe day? (V.E. Day 1945-1995).

I didn't have to look very far to find more than were needed for I am still using many of them. It also gave me the idea for this months article - a reminiscence of the tools used on the farm and the methods of cultivation employed during those war time years.

Most of them had slowly evolved since farming began, in fact for over five thousand years, yet the majority have disappeared or been displaced during the last fifty years.

Looking back the biggest difference in those wartime days was that most of the work was done by hand and most of the land was worked with horses. Horses needed harnesses and almost every large village or small town had a 'saddler and harness maker' where leather work that had disintegrated with wear and tear could be repaired or renewed.

'Artificials' were expensive and used sparingly; the best fertiliser was reckoned to be 'the farmer's foot'! Most farms had a steady supply of well-rotted manure, from the deep strawed bullock yards where it had been trodden in over winter, to the 'midden' - the manure heap - in the centre of the farmyard where the dung from the cows and horses, pigs and poultry, household and garden waste were piled ever higher.

This steaming mass of manure was loaded into two wheel 'tumbrils' (horse carts) with short handled forks. The matted mess was removed layer by layer from the top downwards to make the work easier. The manure was first cut into sections with a two-handed razor sharp knife with wide serrations.

MANURE KNIFE

In the field the manure was removed from the tumbril with a muck krome, a long handled fork with its four tines bent at right angles. It was put into heaps five and a half yards apart and left to further decompose for about a fortnight, then it was scattered around and spread evenly over the ground with a fork. A wonderfully warming job especially on a cold and frosty morning. The field was then ploughed and harrowed with horses, ready for sowing.

If there was any squitch or running grass, this was enemy weed number one, it would smother and choke any crop it competed with. Its long trailing underground roots were worked to the surface, raked into heaps, carted off and dumped if wet or burnt if sufficiently dry. It gave off a most unusual hazy blue smoke. The resultant ashes were very good for the soil. Cereals were sown with a many spouted corn drill which looked like a long box with lots of small organ pipes dragging on the ground beneath it - simply because that was what was used when it was first invented. Any gaps in the rows caused by a blockage or running out of seed would be the talk of the neighbourhood so they were hidden as soon as possible by re sowing the row or the area with a 'gapping' drill.

Grass seeds were broadcast, that is they were scattered evenly by hand in rhythm with the sower walking - just as corn had previously been. An alternative method was a rapidly rotating disc operated at waist level with a leather-thonged bow, in a similar manner to playing a violin, which is why that type of sower was called a 'fiddle'.

Pre-sprited potatoes were dibbled into ploughed ground or dropped by hand into the bottom of manured ridges. The ridges were split by a plough with a double mouldboard which covered the seed on each side and left a furrow in between. Potatoes were soiled up several times during the season to cover and smother weeds and to keep daylight from any surface potatoes which would otherwise turn green and poisonous.

Root crops were sown thinly in rows. The tiny emerging seedlings were gapped or spaced to about every eight inches by hand hoe. This task was often set on a 'piece work' basis and could be continued long after the normal farming day had finished to obtain a bit of extra pocket money and complete the job faster.

To keep the weeds in check the crop was hand-hoed between the plants and by horse hoe along the rows several times during the season.

The farmer often carried a special walking stick with a sharp metal blade on the bottom called a 'thistle spudder'. On seeing a weed, especially a thistle, he would plunge the blade into the soil severing the tap root and hopefully killing it.

Later in the season the crops were 'walked' to remove the weeds, gangs of workers in line abreast would pull up clumps of tall green wild oats, yellow flowering charlock, red poppies and providing they were wearing gloves, blue flowering thistles. The weeds were put into sack 'aprons' tied around the workers waists and the spoil from each crossing of the field was dumped at the headland under the hedge.

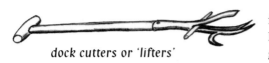

dock cutters or 'lifters'

Docks were dug up with a two pronged fork which had a rounded fulcrum for extra leverage, like a larger version of the gardener's daisy and dandelion lifter for weeding the lawn.

Bogs of nettles and thistles on grazing grass were cut with a scythe. It always seemed a terribly tiring and depressing task but this was largely because it was invariably done on hot stormy, depressing days when the weather was too changeable for haymaking. Grass destined for hay was only scythed on slopes or corners too steep or awkward for horses.

During the war most farmers had a reciprocating-knife grass mower with a long wooden connecting rod which would sometimes snap. It was later replaced by a metal one - that bent! One of the frequent problems was mouse nests which would become impaled on the end of the protruding fingers of the cutter bar. The horses had to be halted, the mower put out of gear and the nest removed every time it happened.

Another drawback was the necessity to keep the triangular sections of the knife blade sharp. A file or carborundum was used to renew the edge of forty cutting surfaces on a five foot blade - held rigid in the field on a special trestle or clamped to the top bar of the gate.

The cut grass was either horse tedded or hand raked to turn the swathes over to dry the underside. When dry it was hand raked into rows or horse raked with multi-pronged curved bars that could be lifted by a lever to let the collected hay fall into a long and continuous row.

It could then be pulled to a stack being built in the field by a two horse hay sweep, otherwise it was loaded onto hay wains, four wheeled carts with long handled two pronged forks called pikels.

For these lighter loads the carrying capacity of the wagons was increased by the addition of harvest ladders, rippling or gawmers, as they were variously called in different areas. They extended the body of the cart or tumbril well over the horse at the front and about an extra four feet at the rear.

Before the corn harvest all the binder canvasses that moved the cut corn to the knotting mechanism were taken to the saddlers shop to have tears and hems stitched and loose slats re-riveted. Corn sheaves were stood like the letter 'A' in shocks, kivvers, mows, stooks or shoofs, all dialect terms for them, and left standing to ripen for three weeks before being carted home to the stackyard.

The stacks had to settle for a fortnight before being thatched with straw. Should rain threaten before either the hay or corn stacks were thatched or a loaded wagon had to be sheeted up overnight, or in a downpour, we used 'tilts' or 'tarpaulins' - water proofed tarred canvasses.

These too went to the saddler periodically to be restitched if torn and new eyelets inserted to fasten the holding ropes, otherwise the wind would get underneath them and blow them away like large kites - which even with the greatest of care some did.

The straw thatch was held in place with strings to broaches, wood sticks about three foot long pushed into the stack.

These were replaced using thatching needles which knotted the straw to the corn sheaves underneath - that was one tool I was able to find that I hadn't used for nearly forty years.

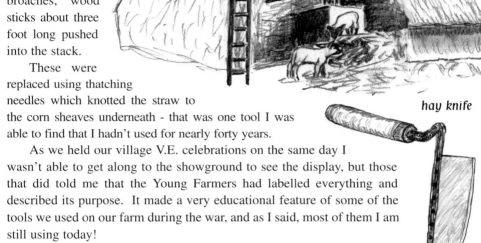

hay knife

As we held our village V.E. celebrations on the same day I wasn't able to get along to the showground to see the display, but those that did told me that the Young Farmers had labelled everything and described its purpose. It made a very educational feature of some of the tools we used on our farm during the war, and as I said, most of them I am still using today!

169 June Bees
'....AND THEIR HIVES OF HISTORY'

I expect you have heard the saying 'A swarm of bees in May is worth a load of hay, a swarm of bees in June is worth a silver spoon, a swarm of bees in July isn't worth a fly' and wondered why. Well there's a lot more to bees and beekeeping than meets the eye as anyone who has an apiary or even a hive will soon tell you.

Bees, honey and nectar all have very ancient and sometimes religious connections. Nectar was the drink of the Gods that made them immortal and gave its name to nectarines which when fully ripe and freshly picked are as sweet as nectar.

The Greek God Zeus was reputedly reared on a mixture of goats' milk and honey and Jupiter was nourished by bees. Honey was once thought to be the product of the Gods, it was their tears which fell to earth that were gathered by the bees. Long before it was realised that honey came from flowers it was also believed that bees flew to Paradise to collect it from the celestial garden.

One of the earliest records of bee-keeping is to be found in an Egyptian Sun Temple near Cairo about 2,400 BC. In addition to eating it as food the Egyptians used it to help embalm their dead and put pots of it in the tomb for the departing soul to feed upon. The honey in these jars was still edible and retained its scent and taste after 3,000 years.

From the Bible comes the story of Samson and his riddle, 'Out of the eater came forth meat and out of the strong came forth sweetness'. The answer can be found in Judges 14. If you haven't a Bible handy you will find the answer on a Lyles Golden Syrup tin, with the extra coincidence that the word 'honey' is of Germanic origin and means 'Golden'.

During the Bronze Age beeswax was essential to their method of casting - the lost wax process. It was also used for religious candles and tapers; beeswax burns with a pleasant aroma and a gentle hum and has been used in most forms of worship ever since.

Hippocrates, the father of medicine, associated honey with longevity, a fact borne out by Phoenician copper and tin traders who stated that the ancient Britons ate so much honey that Britain was referred to as the 'Isle of Honey', where the inhabitants only began to grow old at one hundred and twenty years of age.

Perhaps that is the reason monks became so adept at fermenting honey into mead and why in Scotland a favourite tipple known as 'Atholl Brose' was made of equal proportions of honey, cream and whisky. It is said that Mohammad allowed bees into paradise as they were associated with the soul. I also remember a poem which if I've got it right goes - 'Blest be the bees of Paradise, who do the work of Jesus Christ. Do the work which no man can. God made bees and bees make honey, God made man and man makes money'.

In bygone days bees were never bought or sold, they were always bartered, the exchange rate was for a sack of wheat or flour. Honey was also used as an ancient payment of rent. Wild bees combs hang from trees, and early bee-keepers owned tree colonies and fixed hollow logs to entice them in.

In medieval times straw rope was coiled and held together with split lengths of brambleberry (blackberry), they were called bee skeps. If the straw became wet it would lose its insulation so extra protection was provided by placing a large upturned earthenware bowl on top or placing the skeps in sheltered south facing recesses in brick walls (or tree trunks) called bee boles. Straw keps had the advantage of being warm in winter and cool in summer but the disadvantage was that when the honey was removed the bees were evicted and the colony generally died of starvation.

It wasn't until the 17thC that advances in cabinet-making brought about the use of wooden boxes for housing bees. But the big breakthrough came in 1852 when Lorenzo Langstroth, a Minister in the USA designed a new type of hive with inner removable sections for rearing young bees and separate compartments for the storage of honey and pollen.

Although it was possible to purchase sugar from the Middle East from the 7thC it wasn't until the 17thC that it was widely grown in the New World. Until then honey was not only the main sweetener but it was also far cheaper, a pound of honey sweetened as much as three pounds of sugar.

From early times it was known that honey was a great healer, it is an antiseptic, it was applied to boils, scalds and wounds and when used in conjunction with cobwebs would staunch the flow of blood. It was given to newborn children to protect them from evil and to enhance their chances of survival.

Honey provides instant energy. It was, and still is, used by athletes and Sherpa porters derive their strength from it when climbing the Himalayas.

You don't believe all this? Then what do people do when they get married? They go on 'honeymoon'. In olden days this meant living on a diet consisting largely of honey to give them the extra energy they required for the period of a moon (a month). Honey was also believed to be an aphrodisiac.

But as with bees so with some marriages, they may have honey in their mouths but they also have stings in their tail. It is a fact that people who dislike or are frightened of bees are usually the most likely to get stung, bees seem to sense their disapproval and once they've got you on the run, they'll keep you on the run, for when a bee stings it emits a scent that rouses all the other bees into action.

Again, unfortunately for the bee, its sting is barbed and when it is used it breaks off causing the bee to die. To keep bees placid they were always treated as part of the family. They were told of births, marriages and deaths otherwise they might swarm away and leave, or pine away and die on the death of the owner; which is behind the expression 'Tell it to bees'.

Bees become agitated when confronted by people wearing dark clothing which is why the bee-keeper's suit is white. It is also smooth so that the bees do not get entangled in the fibres. They also become aggressive during hot, dry weather when the nectar will not flow, and against anyone who wears strong smelling perfume, soap or aftershave, or has recently handled horses or goats.

The tried and tested way to quieten them is to puff smoke upon them, smouldering rotten elm is considered the best. The frightened bees gorge themselves on honey and with full stomachs become quite subdued.

At its peak at the end of June and through July a hive might well contain sixty to eighty thousand bees. They become congested, there is no room left for brooding the young or storing pollen and honey. Something has to be done to reduce the overcrowding. Preparations are put in hand by the colony. About a dozen queen cells and several drone cells are capped over, they will provide a future queen for bees that remain behind in the hive. Scouts are sent out to scour the surrounding area for a suitable site for a new home. They return and 'dance' to inform the colony of their findings.

Bees prefer a sheltered site to an exposed one, a dry area to a damp one and refuse to accept any place that may be flooded during heavy rain or is likely to be invaded by honey stealing ants. Prudent bee-keepers often place an empty hive or two on a suitable spot to entice a swarm.

Once the bees have chosen the best site they have to wait for the right weather. From mid-morning to mid-day on a hot and sunny day an increasing number of bees start buzzing excitedly around the hive. They have gorged themselves full of honey and their noise is awesome as a column of some thirty thousand bees swirl around creating a spiralling, moving cloud. The old, slimmed down queen is somewhere among them, as they swoop off to a nearby branch and cling together in a great inverted conical mass. The scouts report back that the chosen site is still vacant, then suddenly the swarm disperses and make a 'bee-line' for their new home.

Behind them, banging on pots and pans, kettles and drums, anything that makes a noise, follow the beekeeper and his family 'tinging the bees'. This was the recognised method of claiming the swarm and gave a right of trespass over other peoples land. When I was a lad I well remember chasing a neighbour's swarm on my bicycle, continually tinging my bell. they fled faster than I could pedal but I kept them in sight and claimed them for him when they settled in a hedge a couple of miles away. In the evening he went and tapped them into an old straw basket, he wasn't wearing protective clothing or even a veil and he never got stung once.

Now to answer the opening quotation - I leave you to solve Samson's riddle.

A swarm of bees in May is worth a load of hay. The explanation is that an early swarm is very valuable, because the swarming bees and those remaining in the hive have time to establish colonies which will yield a good quantity of virgin honey in the autumn and there will be enough left over to feed them through the winter. Well worthwhile.

A swarm of bees in June is worth a silver spoon. With luck and a good season both the swarm and the hive may put down sufficient stores of pollen and honey to see them through the coming winter but it is unlikely there will be honey to spare. Just worth the effort and about the value of a silver spoon.

A swarm of bees in July isn't worth a fly. Even feeding them lots of sugar and water they are unlikely to lay down sufficient food for the winter and will almost certainly perish. They are not worth bothering about - not even worth a fly.

I hope that has helped to explain yet another of our country sayings. I will get around to write about the fascinating life cycle of the busy bee another time.

170 July Bicycles
'MY YEARS IN THE SADDLE'

If I were to tell you that when I was young I spent several hours each week 'in the saddle', it would probably conjure up a mental picture of me riding on a horse.

Well I'm sorry to disappoint you but my saddle days were caused by the necessity of travelling first to school and later to work on my bicycle. It took me about an hour to cycle the eight miles to school six mornings a week and about the same time to return home.

On leaving school I started work as an engineering apprentice and that too was an hour's ride away. Three evenings a week I cycled home, washed, changed, snatched some tea, then cycled back for a couple of hours of further education. It took five years of pedalling to gain my diploma and I never needed it, for after a spell in the forces I left engineering to become a farmer.

Certainly for me and many of my generation, the bicycle was a cheap and reliable means of getting about, so this month I will delve into its history.

The word 'bicycle' comes from the Greek and simply means 'two wheels'. Apart form having a connecting bar of wood, sometimes shaped like a horse, with a wheel between the front legs, another between the rear legs and a padded saddle on top, that was exactly what the earliest machines of the 1790s were - two wheels.

There was no steering, it had to be dragged or lifted around corners. To gain momentum the seated rider had to push his feet against the ground, either together in a swinging motion or alternatively as if striding along.

On a level surface it was much faster than walking and dangerously fast going downhill. The biggest drawback was that it had to be pushed or carried up even a slight incline. It was an expensive toy that gave the young beaux of Byron's day plenty of exercise.

In France the machine was called a 'Celeripeda', in England a 'hobby horse' or a 'dandy horse' after the dressed up 'dandies' of the Regency period, for whom the correct riding attire was a top hat, wing collars and tailcoats.

In 1815 a German, Baron Drais de Sauarbon, improved it with armrests and a bar to steer the front wheel. This machine was called a 'Draisienne' after him.

It, too, became popular with the nobility but not with furious farriers or brawny blacksmiths, who according to several accounts, chased riders and smashed their machines. They were infuriated because 'hobby horses' did not need

DRAISIENNE - HOBBY-HORSE

shoeing and if the idea caught on, it would put them out of business.

Yet ironically, it was a Scottish blacksmith who made the first self-motivated machine. He used long swinging levers, operated by the feet at the front, to turn cranks attached to the rear wheel, a principle still used in some 'go-carts' for children today. A Glasgow paper reported that he was fined five shillings for furious driving in 1842.

It was a Frenchman, Pierre Michaux, who in 1860 had the ingenious idea of putting a grindstone handle on each side of the front wheel and turning the wheel with the feet. Because it could travel four times faster than walking it was call a 'Velocipede', which means 'swift feet'.

In 1868 the French agent for the Coventry Sewing Machine Company brought a velocipede home with him to England. The managing director called his foreman, an inventive genius, James Starley, destined to become the Father of the bicycle, George Singer (later cycles and cars), William Hillman - of cycle and car fame - all into the yard to witness his nephew ride the new fangled French machine.

VELOCIPEDE-BONESHAKER

On seeing the young man leap onto the Velocipede, Starley immediately invented an extension of the rear axle as a step to make mounting easier by more mature people like himself. The firm started producing bicycles and demand rapidly out stripped supply,

'Velocipedemania' gripped the world and Coventry became the cycle manufacturing centre of the world, giving the old city a boost after the collapse of its silk ribbon industry in the face of fierce French competition.

A popular Music Hall song of the day helped sum up some of the dangers of cycling; 'Velocipede, velocipede, the name I can't abide. Although of course it ain't a horse - it's a terrible thing to ride'. A mad dog can be avoided because it runs straight at you, but a madman on a Velocipede runs anything but straight.

Because it had hooped iron wheels and no springs it bumped and jarred over the rough roads and soon gained the reputation of being a 'Boneshaker', a name which, just like the dust from the road, stuck to it forever after.

Since each rotation of the pedals caused the front wheel to turn once, it followed that the larger the wheel, the greater would be the distance travelled. Consequently the front wheel was made bigger and bigger and bigger until it stood some five feet high. Meanwhile, the rear wheel diminished in size to about 18 inches. To the jovial countryman it looked like a farthing chasing a penny, which is exactly why our great, great grandfathers christened it a 'Penny Farthing'.

Again, because of the rough roads the rider needed to be an acrobat as well as an athlete to stay in the saddle. Falls were frequent and coming a cropper by going head over heels caused many a lasting headache. However, in spite of the dangers, high speeds could be attained.

PENNY FARTHING

The guard of one coach and horse team was heavily fined for throwing an iron ball into the wheel of a penny farthing. In court he stated that he lost his temper because the cyclist was overtaking him, even though his horses were galloping flat out.

Because the penny farthing was so difficult to mount, to start, to stop and to control, in 1885 James Starley developed a 'safety' bicycle called the 'Rover'. It had wheels of almost equal size, a tubular frame with a crossbar and a pedal driving a chain to a cog wheel at the rear. It caused a sensation, it heralded the demise of all clumsy, 'ordinary' penny farthings.

STARLING'S SAFETY BICYCL

But the 'Rover' also had problems. It was heavy, tiring to pedal, the cog wheel wore out quickly and it, too, was a 'Boneshaker'. Solid rubber tyres did little to increase the comfort of the rider.

Help was at hand, for in 1880 came another breakthrough. A veterinary surgeon, who could not ride a bike himself, patented a hollow rubber tube which he inflated with his son's football pump, his name was John Boyd Dunlop. Two years later it was further improved by adding a removable outer cover by a chap with the name of 'Michelin'! Within five years pneumatic tyres had revolutionised cycling. Starley, still inventing, devised tensioning of spokes, saddle springs, tricycles with differential gears - still used on cars. He sold two to Queen Victoria and delivered them personally. Also soon to be added by others were ball bearings, a pawl and ratchet operating freewheel, better brakes, acetylene lamps and dynamos to replace the dimness of candles for night riding, then three and four speed gears allowed gradients to be climbed much easier. Bicycle parts were mass produced in separate factories and assembled by over 50 different makers.

The price of bicycles dropped dramatically from £25 to £4 in 10 years, cycling was now within reach of all. Those who couldn't afford new bought second-hand or made their own from bits and pieces.

Ladies prevented their long voluminous skirts from being blown about by sewing lead beads into the hem and they were protected from getting entangled in the gear wheel by a web of wire from hub to mudguard.

Young ladies wore 'rational clothes' - long jackets, knickerbockers, woollen stockings and a straw hat. Divided skirts or the baggy trousers introduced years earlier by the American Mrs Amelia Bloomers also came into fashion, but the showing of ankles was considered highly immodest.

Ladies who couldn't balance on two wheels rode on tricycles or quadricycles described by one journalist as 'A horseless carriage in which ladies with plenty of pluck can go about alone and steer themselves'.

To use the bicycle for courting the tandem was developed, a bicycle made for two. - originally the riders sat side by side - and made famous by another Music hall song 'Daisy'.

Men cycled in Norfolk jackets, breeches and high woollen socks. At the turn of the century cycling clubs, many patronised by Royalty, sprung up all over the country. Ever increasing crowds of cyclists took to the roads at weekends where they discovered the delights of the freedom of the countryside. They used it as an antidote to the deprivations they endured in the towns and cities during the week.

But, just like the donkey before, the bicycle also became the workhorse of many trades and professionals, when as well as being ridden for pleasure or profit, it became the 'working man's friend' and bearer of his burdens. Postmen used them to convey letters, parcels and telegrams post haste. Butchers, bakers and grocers employed whistling errand boys to deliver their wares. One enterprising fire station crew manned a four man quadricycle fully equipped with hoses to speed to the scene of local fires. Housewives would carry their shopping in wicker baskets attached to the handlebars or hung from the back of the saddle.

Biking became a family way of getting about, small children would ride in a special seat, over either the front or rear wheel of mother's bike whilst up to two older children, feet in stirrups would sit on saddles astride the crossbar of father's bike. It was quite a common sight until motor cycles and then motor cars took over the conveyance of the family.

And who among the older ones of you do not remember the delight of having a spare penny in your pocket and hailing your local 'Stop me and buy one' Wall's ice cream salesman on his tricycle.

Yes, life 'in the saddle' brings back many happy memories for me, as well as being the reason for me having the most polished posterior at my school!

171 August Pests
'A FLYING, CRAWLING, HOPPING PLAGUE'

Every season produces its problems. But what is different about this summer is that so many pests have reached plague proportions within such a short space of time.

The first inkling of anything unusual started when the waste water from our upstairs shower wouldn't drain away. My wife had been reminding me for ages that it was getting slower and slower but as usual I had done nothing about it, hoping the problem would go away.

Well it didn't, 'never mind it'll only be a few hairs blocking the U bend', I thought. After removing several floor boards and spending an uncomfortable hour or so on my back, the joints eventually came apart and to my surprise the U bend was as clean as a whistle.

'It must be blocked further down the pipe', I thought. More floorboards came up and another length of pipe was removed, that too was clean. 'Perhaps it's where the pipe bends outside', I thought. Up the wall I went on my ladder, undid the joints, the bend was as clear as a bell.

'Must be the length to the bottom bend', I thought, no blockage there. It was my wife who discovered the cause of the problem, the remaining foot of drainpipe that I hadn't checked was full of SNAILS. About twenty of them were coagulated together, completely sealing the pipe, we had to smash their shells to make a way through. They had crawled up the pipe where it was wet and warm to escape the winters cold but had perished from the heat of the hot water and the soapy sludge.

After replacing the pipes and floorboards we checked the outlets to the other bedroom washbasins which had also been slow to flow, and sure enough there were snails blocking the final foot of every one.

Well, forewarned is forearmed. We had just planted several hundred bedding plants and the seeds were germinating unevenly in the vegetable garden, could it be the snails were eating them and causing them to disappear overnight? The evening was damp and mild, we went into the garden to search for snails.

Within an hour we had collected a hundred and fifty in a plastic bucket. They were crawling up the slippery sides trying to escape. We fed them to our hens and geese. They gobbled them up excitedly at first but soon became 'fed up' with such an enormous quantity of delicacies. Over the next week we accounted for over fifteen hundred.

This year our seedlings and plants have not had to combat the ravages of an abundance of slugs and snails and until this recent hot spell had grown outstandingly well, and all as a result of that waste pipe being blocked. An additional bonus is that we have had far fewer 'slugs' nibbling at our lettuces. For to my mind there is only one thing worse than finding a slug in your lettuce when eating it, and that is finding HALF a slug and wondering what happened to the other half!

Earlier in the year I had moved and repainted a greenhouse and disturbed the hibernation of hundreds of 'ladybirds'. There will be no problem with greenfly or blackfly this year as each can consume several hundred aphids in a season, I thought. How wrong I was to be proved.

Black fly had almost smothered the few docks and thistles I removed from my fields last month and they were gathering thickly on the tender tips of the broad beans when we picked the tops off. Greenfly had so inundated the roses that the buds were starved of sap and become deformed or wilted away and there wasn't a ladybird to be seen.

However the prolonged heat wave that we are at present experiencing has stopped the plants shooting, starved of sap the greenfly have dehydrated into extinction. In contrast the ladybirds have proliferated to such an extent that they are swarming around and, finding no aphids to feed upon, are biting people in their desperate attempt to find food.

Another insect that preys on greenfly is the ant. It tickles the greenfly with its feelers to induce it to excrete a droplet of sugar sap 'honeydew'.

Sometimes lots of it falls onto the lower leaves of oaks and limes creating a shiny, sticky, sugary film on them and on pavements or cars parked underneath. During the summer black moulds feed on the sugars and darken the leaves.

Ants find this honeydew so attractive that they often confine greenfly in silicon and saliva 'cowsheds' built on the plant stems and regularly extract the honeydew or 'milk them' as it is termed - just as we do cows.

If you have ever accidentally sat on an ants' nest on the lawn, you will know they also have a vicious means of defence 'formic acid', which can be extremely painful.

Young queens and males waiting to mate, grow wings. The worker ants keep them in the nest until conditions are right. Then the nest erupts and out fly thousands of energetic males and queens. Suddenly the air is filled, not only with swarms of flying ants, but also with dozens of whirling birds and screaming seagulls who somehow sense the prospect of an easy meal. But there are so many airborne pests that the birds soon eat their fill and just like my hens and geese, they too become 'fed up'.

For the past hour our ginger tom cat 'Jasper' has been curled up, purring away on my lap. On the edges of his ears are several small dark dots sucking his blood - fleas - in spite of being regularly dusted against them. This year the number of reported cases have reached plague proportions. They say that for every five you see there are a thousand more hiding in the cushions and carpets waiting their chance to jump onto passing pets. Warm winters, centrally heated houses, wall to wall carpets and soft furnishings are all thought to play a prominent part in their dramatic increase.

Probably our most widely feared pest is the wasp. Fertile queens hibernate in hollow trees, loft spaces or behind bedroom curtains. In the spring the one per cent that survive chew wood to make a dome shaped paper nest in a discarded mouse hole or roof cavity and lay a dozen or so eggs.

Many a time I've seen queen wasps catch a caterpillar as it dangles in mid air on its silken thread from the partly consumed leaves of an oak tree. With a well aimed bite the queen paralyses the caterpillar then carries it home to the nest to feed her larvae.

After about five weeks the larvae become adult workers and take over caring for the future young. The queen continues laying eggs, some twenty five thousand or so in a season.

By August male wasps and new queens are hatched, the old queen has had enough and no more eggs are laid. The multitude of workers enlarging the nest, building combs, collecting flies and insects, feeding the young, all become redundant.

Freed from their domestic chores the social structure and discipline of the nest breaks down and its every wasp for itself. They go on the rampage searching for food wherever they can find it which is why they suddenly become such a nuisance.

Last weekend in the heat of our village fete we were inundated by hordes of them. They were after everything edible, sweet or with moisture. Those who tried to stop them got stung. During the afternoon many people got fed up with them and the hot sun and went home early. We have since disposed of several nests. Nowadays we do it with lethal powders but in my young days by plunging a burning paraffin soaked rag into the nest at dusk. Nests not destroyed by man or badgers are usually abandoned by late summer. The individual wasps die of over intoxication after eating fermented fruit juices, or from exposure on frosty autumn nights.

As I write I'm watching the cycle of yet another pest starting to unfold. Dozens of cabbage white butterflies are gathering nectar on our buddleia bush, some are mating. The females are flying down to lay their eggs on the underside of the nasturtium leaves that have grown so prolifically since we killed the slugs and snails. Soon I shall have another job - removing the pungent odoured caterpillars from the leaves of the nasturtiums!

Yes, life is seldom without its problems and this year we certainly appear to have suffered from our full share. What with slugs and snails, black fly, greenfly, ants, ladybirds, fleas, wasps and caterpillars we seem to have had the lot - but there again I could be wrong!!

172 September Old Measures
'IT'S GOODBYE TO THEM...'

It's on its way. Within a few days another piece of Brussels beaurocracy will permanently put an end to most of the weights and measures that we have used for generations.

The shopkeeper will no longer legally be able to sell us a pound of jam nor the farm shop a half hundredweight bag of potatoes. Instead they will have to deal in grams and kilos. When I buy a new shirt the collar size will be 40 centimetres not the $15^{1/2}$ inches that I have used all my adult life. Many goods are already double labelled, in future metric will have to be the dominant one on display.

For the young the change will be absorbed almost without notice. The middle aged will probably have to pause and put the new price into perspective when shopping but their minds are still agile enough to accept the change. Those of us who are past our 'sell by' date will probably never fully get used to it. We shall always tend to compare the new measures with those indoctrinated into us by repetition at school.

Since to my mind 'metrication' has no bearing on reality except that it is divisible by ten, I thought this might be a suitable time to explain how some of our weights and measures came into existence and how some of them changed or became obsolete to adapt to fresh circumstances. Many measurements were formed from the human frame or the food we ate.

An INCH was the width of a man's thumb; during the 14C Edward II ruled that it should also equal the length of three barley grains placed end to end.

Still used for calculating the height of horses from the ground to the withers (shoulders) is the HAND. Originally it also included the thumb and was five inches. but was later reduced to the width of the palm - four inches.

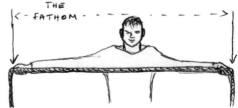

span

One measurement that has disappeared in all but its name is the 'SPAN', the distance of an outstretched hand between the tips of the thumb and little finger which was reckoned to be nine inches.

If I asked you 'how long is a foot?' the reply would almost certainly be twelve inches. But it wasn't always so. it began by being eleven and a half inches. In more ways than one we now have bigger feet than our ancestors.

By ancient law houses in the countryside were built in 'bays' of sixteen feet. This was the width considered necessary to house a team of four oxen side by side. Before measurements were standardised the ruling was that the first sixteen men leaving church on a Sunday each had to place one foot in line on the site. That was then the lawful and legally accepted internal measurement of the bay, byre, stable or room, call it what you will.

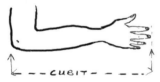

Biblical dimensions. such as the size of the Ark (Genesis 6 v. 15) are given in cubits which was the length from elbow to fingertips, eighteen inches or half a yard.

The YARD itself was originally the length of a man's belt or girdle but to avoid confusion Henry I fixed the yard as being the distance from the nose and outstretched thumb. This 'yardstick' became a very useful measurement for people selling lengths of cloth and for a long time was known as the clothyard.

Arrowshafts were described as being of 'clothyard length', since when the bowstring was drawn back its full distance to the nose, the bow, held at arms length. required an arrowshaft a yard long.

An interesting development from the yard was the FATHOM the distant from thumb tip to thumb tip of outstretched arms, which gave two yards or six feet. Sailors used this method to 'fathom the depths' with a thin lead-weighted line - so also called 'plumbing the depths'. On the Mississippi river boatmen called a fathom 'mark one' and two fathoms 'mark twain' - the pseudonym of the writer Samuel Clemens.

To estimate the speed of a ship at sea, knots were tied in the 'log' line run out in the wake and timed with a sand glass. Twenty knots was twenty nautical miles per hour and just to confuse the issue this nautical mile is 2027 yards.

Roman distances were marked in 'paces', which was a double step, equal to about five feet. A thousand paces made a Roman mile, 1817 yards.

Before the English MILE was standardised by Elizabeth I at 1760 yards, London, Wales, Scotland and Ireland all had their differing lengths. The Welsh walked the furthest, about four times as far as the English mile.

The distance that a team of oxen could plough a furrow before resting gave us another important indicator of old - a furrowlong - a FURLONG - 220 yards. When divided by ten it gave a CHAIN - 22 yards, the distance between the stumps at cricket.

The chain of 22 yards was further subdivided into four lengths of fifteen and a half feet called a ROD, POLE or PERCH. They marked the important distance that the ploughman turned the soil towards the central furrow before going on to his next stage. Until the introduction of the one-way plough the rod, pole or perch measurement produced the most efficient and economical way of ploughing a field.

The length of a furrow - 220 yards - multiplied by the distance between the furrows - 22 yards - gives the area known as an acre. Even that is being replaced by its continental cousin the hectare which has no rural meaning to justify its existence.

In my tables at school it was 'drilled' into me that 'eight furlongs make a mile', and with a nine inch furrow the ploughman and his team walked eleven miles to turn over each acre of ground, which was considered a day's work.

Weights were either TROY, from Troyes in France or AVOIRDUPOIS which means the heaviness of objects. The smallest unit was originally a GRAIN (of wheat), seven thousand of which made one POUND. In Elizabeth 1's time this was divided into sixteen OUNCES. A now obsolete term, a PENNYWEIGHT was literally the weight of an old English penny.

In Cheshire the heavier George Ill 'cartwheel' penny was given to the farmer's bride to add to the weights on her butter scales so that she could never be accused of selling short measure. In consequence the coin was locally called a BUTTERPENNY.

Weights could so easily be tampered with by boring holes or removing some of the lead infill that they were tested or assized by inspectors to prevent dishonest dealings. The Worshipful Company of Plumbers tested lead weights, while the Worshipful Company of Founders were responsible for brass and bronze weights. They marked each with a stamp which in Cheshire has the county emblem of wheatsheaves.

The day to day weights used by inspectors were called 'Working Standards' and they were checked against 'Local Standards' held at their office. These in turn were checked with even more accurate ones called 'Imperial Standards'.

Wool was weighed with special shield-shaped cast bronze weights of fourteen pounds. A tax of one penny had to be paid on each TOD of 28lbs. Because metal weights were expensive masons chipped equivalent weights out of stone, at a cheaper price, which is why l4lbs is often calls a STONE.

From the 1850s the Royal Mail introduced special weights to check letters, they were called POSTAGES, while banks had their 'SOVEREIGN' scales and specific weights to balance larger amounts of coinage to save time laboriously counting it out.

Liquid measures were sometimes used for selling solids, you don't believe me, then what about a PINT of shrimps. Garden seeds were mainly measured by volume instead of weight. To try to keep inflation under control wages were once fixed by the price of a GALLON of bread.

And coming back to cereals, my father used to sell his corn in COMBS which was a volume measure of four BUSHELS and varied from 168 lbs for oats to 252 lbs for wheat. A bushel was a round wooden container - the corn was levelled off at the top with a straight wooden bar. This measure succumbed to the two pronged attack of fashion and woodworm.

Even our HUNDREDWEIGHT is not as simple as it sounds; it does not comprise of a hundred pounds as one might assume, but of the 'Long Hundred' avoirdupois of 112 lbs.

As yet unchanged is the CARAT which derives from the weight of the Arabic Karob bean and is used for weighing gold and precious stones. Pure gold is 24 carats. Nine carats denotes nine parts of gold and fifteen of alloy, which is not as pure but wears longer.

Yes, the confusion of metrication is on its way. Soon those attractive conical cans that once measured oil on garage forecourts, the gleaming brass bell weights in butchers' shops and the circular weights that fitted pyramid fashion on top of one another on greengrocers scales will be relegated to our memories and become amusing exhibits in museums or at antique fairs, when children will ask, 'What is that, Grandad?'

173 October   Plant reproduction
'SPREADING THE SEEDS OF SUCCESS'

As a result of a good turn I did for someone many years ago, they sent me a little badge with the inscription upon it: 'All the flowers of all our tomorrows are sown in the seeds of today.'

That saying is equally true of the human race as it is of our flora and fauna. Nature is truly marvellous for just as we are singing 'All is safely gathered in' at out Harvest Festivals many of the seeds of plants, flowers, trees and weeds are being dispersed to safeguard the survival of the species.

It is well worth looking into the many ways that plants propagate, the miracle of nature's bounty. In many instances she provides an incentive, a reward to those who distribute her seed. For example, an apple hangs enticingly on a tree, you pick and enjoy the nutritious fruit and throw the core. Those brown pips in the centre now have a remote chance to grow in a new area.

Or you pluck a ripe red plum - that is assuming the wasps haven't got there first - eat the juicy fruit then spit the stone out a few yards further on. That stone stands a greater chance of survival than any that fall to earth underneath the tree and try to grow up in its shadow.

In a similar way rats. mice and squirrels will horde a secret store of acorns, beechmast and nuts in their larder. Occasionally a seed may be dropped en-route, the mammal forgets the site or perishes before eating them, and possibly one seed has an outside chance to grow.

When you stop to consider the reality that an oak tree will only require ONE acorn to survive, germinate, grow and mature every four hundred years to maintain the species it puts the problem into perspective. The rest of the acorns are simply a food incentive, otherwise we would soon be inundated with oak trees.

Birds eat soft fruits, the outer covering is digested as food but the seeds pass through their stomach undigested and are excreted as part of their droppings - some may take root. Mistle thrushes do this with mistletoe berries which occasionally stick to their beak, they wipe them off on a branch and perhaps a few years later a sprig of mistletoe will appear.

Birds can eat poisonous yew berries with impunity because their stomach juices do not dissolve the seed. Animals and human stomach juices are stronger and will release the deadly toxins from the seed, which is one of the reasons yew trees are grown in the fenced area of churchyards where animals cannot reach them.

Any farmer who spreads sewage sludge on his fields will soon be aware of one seed that passes through our stomachs intact - tomatoes. Migrating birds also carry small seeds vast distances in the mud on their feet.

In colder climes such as ours the reward given to those who spread the seed is mainly fleshy such as apples, pears, berries and nuts. In hotter countries their attraction is emphasised by additional moisture as in grapes, water melons, oranges and bananas.

Another common means of seed distribution are the so called 'hangers on'. The barbed seed heads of plants such as burdock whose 'sticky burrs' hitch a ride on fur, feather or clothing. Nature's design of these hooks was the inspiration for the invention of the 'velcro' fastener. As a youngster I well remember my mother spending ages clipping and teasing thick clusters of burrs from our spaniel's coat and hairy ears after returning from rabbit or duck shooting expeditions with dad.

A seed with a smaller but similar action is that of the 'goosegrass' or 'cleavers'. Its country name is 'sweethearts' because boys flicked them at their girlfriends. If they stuck fast she might well become your sweetheart - or give you a thick ear in retaliation. Teazels have such an effective and long lasting hook on their seed case that until quite recently their barbs were used to raise the nap on cloth.

Of course many seeds simply drop to the ground immediately under the parent plant. If the parent dies over winter the new seed can emerge unhindered to take its place the following season. Otherwise the germination will be overshadowed and smothered, the seedlings will grow up sickly and may well die.

Nature has therefore developed an alternative distribution system which makes use of the WIND. Some seeds, such as poppies, stay in the seedhead until the wind shakes them sufficient strongly to dislodge a few seeds at a time from tiny openings just under the conical cap. They fall onto fresh ground a foot or two away.

Trees whose seeds would stand little chance of survival under the canopy of their branches often produce winged seeds which hitch a lift on the breeze and like miniature propellors twirl away from the parent. Some seeds such as ash have a single wing, the sycamore cunningly joins two seeds together so that its double wingspan can propel it even further.

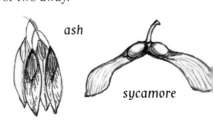

ash

sycamore

Another adaptation using the wind is the seed that is suspended beneath a 'parachute' of hairs. Into this category comes the dandelion 'clock' that children blow to tell the time, also thistledown which with my granny I used to gather in basketfulls to stuff cushions and pillows.

If you have ever had a vase of the spectacular spikes of the greater reed mace or bulrush

overwintering in the hall, and one of them has burst, you will know how easily the fluffy, cotton wool, seeds are dispersed and also how difficult it is to gather them up afterwards. Rose bay willow herb can cover considerable distances. During the war it was one of the first plants to colonise sites devastated by the fire bombs of the blitz, consequently its red flower was called 'fireweed'.

Mushrooms. fungi, ferns and puffballs produce millions of tiny spores that are scattered by the wind, dislodged by falling raindrops or washed away to fresh sites in a storm.

Just as the coconut palm produces a fruit that is buoyant enough to be carried on ocean currents to distant tropical shores so many of our riverside trees have adapted the flow of water to propagate their species. Tiny twigs of willow blown off by strong winds drift downstream. One may become embedded in the bank, take root and mature into a full blown willow tree.

The banks of the stream that run through my meadows are now lined with alders whose corky seeds have floated down during floods. Dense stocking during my early farming years meant that emerging seedlings were eaten before they had a chance to mature. But since the milk quota reduced the number of cows many more seedlings survived and are now small trees.

Rather than rely on wind or water, animals or birds, some plants, such as species of the pea family, propel their progeny several yards by a sudden spring-like popping action of the seed pod. Broom is a well-known example.

Strawberries and creeping buttercups send out overground runners which root where the tip touches the soil, the new plant sends out more runners and so on all to get away from the influence of the parent and set up a new home elsewhere.

Others rely on the 'underground', seeking fresh areas through the expansion of roots or rhizomes. Two very troublesome weeds of this sort are squitch and bindweed (convolvulus).

Bracken uses two methods of reproduction, spores and underground roots that quickly colonise new areas and is extremely difficult to eradicate.

Many species of tree, plums, ash and sycamore, send up 'suckers' from their root system, even oaks will do it after a mature tree is felled - all in the name of survival.

Bluebells, daffodils and most other bulbs increase both by seed and by producing baby bulbs from the mother plant slowly increasing in density and expanding in the area they cover. Others do something similar on the surface: you may well have noticed how quickly a single daisy can spread to become a clump on your lawn.

Once dispersed to a fresh site some seeds can lay dormant for years waiting for conditions to be right before germinating. Our red poppies, the symbol of the slaughter in Flanders, has seeds that will wait a hundred years or more before sprouting, other seeds last even longer.

All of which gives an added emphasis to my opening quotation 'all the flowers of all our tomorrows are sown in the seeds of today'.

'For as with seeds, so with weeds.... and as with rumens, so with humans.'

174 November Lead
'PLUMBING THE DEPTHS OF HEAVY INDUSTRY'

LEAD is probably the most destructive metal ever discovered. It has been mined from parts of our countryside for well over three thousand years, often as a part-time secondary job by moorland and hill farmers to help increase their meagre income. Thousands of dangerous, uncapped and waterlogged shafts or 'rakes' still litter areas where the ore was extracted.

The ancient ruling was that a prospector must mine a 'dish' of fifty-six pounds weight of an ore from a site before he could drive in a stake to claim the site and continue extraction - hence to 'stake a claim'.

Adjacent land was made available for him to erect a hut or house, outbuildings and sheds to work in. He was granted access to water and a right of way to the nearest road. Mining was not allowed under buildings, churchyards, orchards, gardens or the highway. One dish in every thirteen (later one in twenty five) was paid to the crown as tax.

stow
or
stowse

Mines were inspected every three months, if not being worked a 'nick', was cut into the claim stake. If after three visits and three resultant nicks the mine was still derelict the lease lapsed and another claimant could take over, which explains the true origin of the term 'nicked'.

Lead mining was not a job for the faint hearted or weak willed. The miners only light came from a tallow candle stuck to his hat or the walls with soft clay.

Before the days of explosives an average shift of eight hours with pick and shovel might result in two inches of rock face and ore being removed. Unwanted rock was left on the floor as back filling whilst ore from the vein was passed back along the tunnel to the bucket at the bottom of the shaft from whence it was raised to the surface. From 1750 some of the workload was eased by wooden carts which ran on planks - later these were replaced with iron rails and metal wheels. In the main women and older children worked above ground 'dressing' the ore, reducing the rocks to the size of a pea with heavy hammers.

LEAD MINERS BOOT FROM HAZARD MINE NR. BUXTON IT HAD A WOODEN SOLE EDGED WITH IRON

A slurry of rock and ore was poured down a gentle slope. The heavier lead ore settled out at the top, the lighter rock waste ran away. The ore was sold to the smelters, and payment was made about every six weeks in one of the many pubs in the area. '

The ore was smeltered on charcoal fires and hilltop boles to catch the wind, later water wheels and bellows provided the continuous blast of air required to heat the furnace.

The gunpowder of those days included 'saltpetre' (potassium nitrate). When a vein became so poor it would no longer cover the cost of the gunpowder and the work required to remove the ore, it was said to have 'petered out'.

The Latin word for lead is plumbum and Plumb became the surname of those who worked with it around the 13th century, another is Leadbeater.

Masons used a pointed pendulum of lead suspended on a cord to indicate the perpendicular - as we now say a 'plumb-bob' on a 'plumb-line'.

Being nearly twelve times as dense as water lead falls extremely rapidly, in fact it plummets down and because of this was used to 'plumb the depths' of rivers and oceans. It was also because water was conveyed inside lead pipes that the person who installed them was called a plumber. When you think about it he really ought to be called a waterer. To join two lengths of lead pipe together the ends were heated and an alloy of lead and tin added - we call it solder. The resultant bulge was wiped smooth with a soft moleskin leather

Freshly cast or cut lead is bright and shiny but when exposed to the air it soon develops a dark film which obscures its brightness, that is why a dull, grey, overcast day has 'leaden skies'.

A brightening feature for which lead was formerly in great demand was as a pigment for paint, plaster and putty. An unfortunate side effect was lead poisoning, a slow wasting disease inducing a dullness of the brain and partial paralysis, especially of the wrists, to which painters, plumbers, glaziers, smelters or even people living in freshly painted rooms could easily succumb. A wider cause of poisoning among ladies of fashion came from the belief that a pale skin was an indication of superiority and aristocracy. White lead was used as a cosmetic which resulted in a blotchy skin, this in turn was obscured by adding more - a case of adding insult to injury.

In spite of these drawbacks lead had a great many points in its favour. It had a low melting point of $334°C$ and when incorporated with copper, zinc and tin as an alloy it made the bearings on which the shafts of the Industrial Revolution revolved. Its capacity to be rolled, moulded and beaten into almost any shape, even when cold, made it ideal for making waterproof the joints between brickwork and roofing in a form we call 'flashings'. Roof gullies and gutters could be beaten into shape with rounded wooden hammers on site, and being waterproof whole roofs could be clad with a long lasting layer of sheet lead.

This was used extensively on churches and cathedrals, which were frequently the target of thieves when scrap lead prices were high, a theft which often went undiscovered until it rained.

And going inside the church for a moment the pipes of the great organ were made of rolled lead sheets, and a neighbouring church even has a lead-lined font.

Stained glass windows in churches and latticed windows in houses required an 'H' section of lead with soldered joints to hold the panes in place. Around about 1675 it was discovered that adding a proportion of lead to molten glass made it shine with more brilliance and gave greater clarity to optical lenses. The product became known as lead-crystal.

The low melting point coupled with its ease of casting and handling made lead (plus 25% antimony) an ideal material to make letters for the printing press. The operator typed out a line at a time on 'slugs' of hot metal giving it the name 'Lino-type'.

A valuable by-product from some of the early lead ores was a small proportion of silver which made the miner's job slightly more rewarding, a point not overlooked by fraudsters who debased the currency by casting counterfeit coins cheaply using a high content of lead.

Lead was used to line the coffins of the wealthy to exclude the air and delay putrefaction, to keep them looking fresh for longer. Centuries later thin 'lead foil', 'tinfoil', or 'silver paper' as it became known, was used to wrap chocolate, tea and tobacco to keep them fresh. Unfortunately contamination of the contents by the formation of lead oxides was a cause of food poisoning until aluminium foil was substituted.

A lead miner's lamp filled with oil
- a wick burned from the spout

In country houses, water cisterns, sinks and wash troughs were made entirely from lead or were lined with it. Milk was stored in shallow lead pans to allow the cream to rise, settle and be skimmed off to make butter or cheese, and brewery beers were made in lead lined vats. In more recent times lead was used as a ballast for racing yachts and diving outfits.

Concern was expressed when it was found that swans who swallowed lead weights discarded by fishermen became poisoned and many died. There were also many cases of poisoning among itinerant travellers who were burning old car battery cases on their fires to extract the lead.

Lead coverings were used to protect high voltage underground cables from loss of power and used as a shield against radiation especially in hospital X ray departments.

And have you ever wondered how iron railings were 'cemented' into their stone base? The secret was an inverted mushroom shaped hole in the base stone into which molten lead was poured. Take a closer look next time you pass, so simple but so effective. Iron dowels, fastening statues to plinths and grave headstones, were also held upright by this same method.

When young I spent many happy hours playing games with my lead soldiers, fighting imaginary wars with equally brightly coloured Red Indian warriors on horseback. A few years later I spent many more happy hours making and listening on my headphones to my crystal set, the crystal of which was lead spa or galena - lead ore. In those early days of broadcasting it was almost the only way of detecting the electromagnetic radio waves. Was this why the alchemists of old dedicated lead to saturn?

But by far the biggest use for lead has been warfare. Being so dense lead travelled further and more accurately than other metals. Round balls were used by the ancients as sling shot and ammunition for catapults. Boiling lead poured from above was a highly effective deterrent against castle intruders. Musket balls were individually cast or cold pressed from sheet lead with cup-shaped pliers. Small shot was produced by pouring molten lead through a fine sieve and dropping it 150 feet into water in a special shot tower - there is one at Chester.

Before anaesthetics (1850s) injured soldiers had to 'bite the bullet' of soft musket lead to stop them screaming out in pain when the surgeon was amputating limbs.

Of all the metals used through history lead has probably caused the most human deaths through warfare, poisoning and sport.

And now after this hot summer we hear of yet another possible link with lead poisoning to car exhausts through lead used in petrol as an anti-knocking agent. YES lead has taken some knocks over the years, but I am sure it can absorb a few more.

175 December Demon Drink
'HIGH DAYS, HOLY DAYS - ANY EXCUSE TO DRINK'

In days gone by any feast, festival, saint's day or gathering to celebrate a special occasion provided a good excuse to have a drink, either to drown sorrows or to make merry. It temporarily smoothed the harshness of life, for a short while people forgot their problems and enjoyed themselves.

At one time almost every household brewed its own ale. Herbs were added to sharpen the taste. Favourite flavourings were burnt-hay from the centre of spontaneous combustible stacks, bog myrtle, mugwort, wormwood, rosemary or ground ivy - which made a brew called 'ale hoof'.

Hops were introduced from 1520. At first Henry VIII banned their use as he loved spiced ale, but gradually hops took over and 'ale' became 'beer'. To make it, barley was steeped in water to induce it to germinate.

The best brews were made with fresh spring or well water, especially from under chalk, the worst from rain water or peat streams. The developing shoots were slowly dried. The longer the drying the darker the malt and the resultant beer, boiling water was poured on, the porridge was stirred for ten minutes then left to stand for four hours after which the liquid (wort) was drained from the mash. Hops or herbs were added and the wort boiled for about four hours to extract the flavour. When the wort had cooled to milk warmth yeast was added and stirred with a besom broom.

A slice of toast was floated on the surface to attract the yeast. At first the yeast fed on the oxygen, but for further fermentation honey or sugar was added. When 'working' beer was said to be 'on the smile'. It was covered with a blanket to prevent the vinegar-bug entering.

If it should sour a further handful or two of malt was added. The excess yeast was skimmed off and passed on to the next family to brew, no one bought yeast in the countryside.

Further washings of the mash produced progressively weaker brews just like tea. The second was called 'small beer', it was less intoxicating and was used for farmworkers especially at harvest time, they could drink plenty without becoming befuddled. It was carried to the fields in small barrels called 'costrels' which contained about four pints.

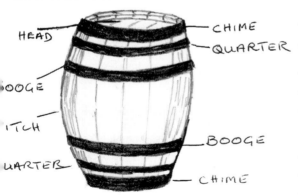

The third rinse provided beer that was used at mealtimes and could be drunk by children without ill effect.

When the brew had matured in barrels for a week or so the broom with which it had been stirred was hung outside to signify the new brew was for sale, the forerunner of our inn signs.

Neighbours called in to sample the brew. They dipped crusts of bread in for good luck, this was called 'taking the shot'. Although sometimes supervised by the men, brewing was usually done by the womenfolk as part of their household chores. If the wives also sold the brew they were known as 'Alewives'.

In London 'Ale-silver' was an annual payment given to the Lord Mayor for the privilege of selling ale in the city.

Official 'Ale-tasters' also went round testing against excessive sugar or other adulteration. They poured a small amount onto a wooden seat and sat on it. If the ale had too high a sugar content it solidified and stuck their leather trousers to the seat, in which case the brewer was hauled before the magistrate then pilloried, fined, or as at Chester, strapped into the ducking stool and lowered under the water several times. 'Ale-tasters' also awarded prizes at the annual fairs, a red ribbon for the best brew and a blue one for the runner up.

The strongest brew of the year, called 'Old October' was made from the new malt of harvest, it matured to be drunk at Christmas. On wintry nights ale or beer was warmed in a 'muller', a copper cone or shoe shape whose point or toe was put into the embers of the fire.

Another method was to plunge a red hot poker into the tankard. A favourite drink at Christmastide was Lambswool, roasted apples floating on spiced mulled wine and topped with whipped cream. it probably derived from the ancient custom of passing round the 'wassail' bowl from which everyone would drink deeply for good health and divine protection. The original words 'waes hael' in fact meant good health.

In some cider orchards a ceremony called wassailing still continues. The assembled throng blow their horns and fire guns through the branches of the trees to scare away any lurking evil spirits. A piece of cider-soaked toast is placed on the fork of a chosen tree and a pail-full of cider is poured over the roots as a tribute to Pamona the goddess of the orchard. She is then toasted and sung to in rhyme in the hope of a bumper crop the following season.

When farmworkers wages were partly paid in kind, cider was more economical than beer because barley could be sold at the market. Made between November 1 and Christmas, the windfall apples were pulped in a round stone trough under heavy stone rollers. The pulp was pressed, the residue 'pomace' was used as a cattle food, the liquid apple juice over-wintered in wooden barrels. The resultant rough cider was drunk from pint mugs filled from two gallon jugs. The Somerset name for it was 'Tanglefoot' because that is what it did to you on your way home.

An old saying to be observed by drinkers was 'beer on cider makes bad rider but cider on beer brings good cheer'. Apart from making mead from honey, monks also brewed beer for sale. To show that it was of the highest quality they religiously branded their casks with a cross 'X'. After the dissolution of the monasteries the sign of the X was used by the excise to denote barrels of high quality beer on which the excise duty had been paid.

Although the almost indestructible horn beaker was widely used, the best vessel from which to drink was reckoned to be a pewter mug kept at the same temperature as the beer. Stitched leather tankards, made leakproof with a lining of pitch, were called 'Black-jacks'. Glass bottomed tankards were introduced in press gang areas so that drinkers could see an 'enemy' approaching even as they drank. It also helped to prevent downing the contents after anyone had slipped the 'King's shilling' into it, for that meant acceptance of conscription into the army. Both these reasons are why we still say 'bottoms up' before draining the glass.

The word 'bumper' - a plentiful crop - has an even stranger derivation. In Roman times men drank the health of their mistress by downing a 'bumper', an overflowing glass of wine to each letter of her name, a case of inebriated admiration especially if she had a long name.

This too has come down to us in the saying 'Bumpers all round and no heel taps'. In other words, everyone's glass has to be filled to the brim and no one is to pour it into the pot plant!

Equally amusing is the reason why we raise our glasses and propose a 'toast'. In tankards and loving cups a piece of toast was floated to improve the flavour. During the reign of Charles II in the city of Bath a beautiful lady was taking the waters in the Public Baths. An admirer dipped his glass into the water, raised it up for all to see, then drank her health. Almost immediately another admirer, rather the worse for wear jumped into the water and said he didn't care for the water but he would have the 'toast' meaning the lady herself. A story which reminds me of the name given to the first drink known to man, 'Adam's Ale' - water.

To mix our beers and alter the taste we ask for 'mild and bitter'. London street porters mixed three grades, at first called 'Entire' but later 'Porter' after their trade. 'Beer Money' was payment of a penny a day given to soldiers instead of an issue of beer, nowadays it refers to spending money. Sailors received a daily ration of rum and an extra ration if they had accomplished a very difficult task such as 'splicing the mainbrace'.

In 1740 Admiral Vernon, to reduce both costs and alcoholism, watered down the rum ration. Because he wore a grogram coat he was nicknamed 'Old Grog', the rum ration became 'Grog' and those who drank too much became 'groggy'.

Incidentally, the rum ration continued until 1971 when it went 'down the hatch'. Although ale, beer and cider were the daily sustenance of the working man, wine was the prerogative of the rich. It came from vineyards in Britain and British vineyards in France, parts of which were a colony until 1451.

When the Navigation Act of 1651 made wine very expensive people searched for, and soon found, a cheaper alternative - 'spirits'. It was a widely held belief that everything contained a living spirit within it. In wine the distilled essence was said to contain the spirit but it was extremely expensive. The breakthrough came when it was discovered that cereal grains could be distilled into spirit form and become 'whiskey', or 'gin', named after the added flavouring, juniper berries of Geneva.

These alcoholic grain 'spirits' were so cheap they were advertised as 'drunk for a penny, dead drunk for tuppence', and led to the infamous scene in the incriminating picture of depravity 'Gin Lane' by Hogarth. The rich drank wine by the bottle - many emptied four bottles a day, and as a consequence they frequently suffered from bouts of gout. 'Port' was so called because it was shipped from Oporto in Portugal.

But life was not 'all beer and skittles'. Demon drink was responsible for unpaid rent, underfed children, brawls and blasphemy, rape and pillage, gambling and the gallows, and a movement against drinking was formed called the 'Band of Hope' which tried to help drunkards reform and promise to abstain from alcohol.

They had to sign the 'pledge' and keep the card by them as a constant reminder. Weekly meetings were held in chapels, halls and schools where concerts, magic lantern shows and lectures would warn of the evils of drink. One such speaker, Dick Turner of Lancashire, stuttered and when he demanded t-t-t-total abstinence, the 't' caught the imagination of his audience and ever after they were known as 'T-totalers'.

In 1830 William IV abolished the tax on beer and spirits, anyone could open a beer shop for a fee of two guineas and forty-five thousand responded. Then twenty two years later Gladstone cut the tax on tea and gradually it became the national drink.

The 'Band of Hope' played on with a choir of six thousand voices in the Crystal Palace to demonstrate the strength of feeling and to try to persuade Parliament to prohibit the sale of alcohol. The peers in the House of Lords were mocked - it was called 'The House of the Beerage'.

The growth of leisure pursuits and pastimes has meant that ale, beer and cider, wines and spirits have slowly become recreational drinks to be enjoyed, not over indulged, especially on special occasions.

Rabbit hutch or goose fattening cage using an old barrel

So 'God rest ye merry...' this Christmastide, and don't overdo the demon drink.

1996

176 January 'Iron' Rations
'HOW NAPOLEON KEPT FOOD FRESH'

It was about two hundred years ago that Napoleon the French Emperor said 'An army marches on its stomach'. He knew that even the best trained and bravest soldiers had to be well fed to win battles.

But there was a problem. Most fruits and vegetables had to be eaten in their season, there was no efficient way of storing them. Meat too had to be consumed within a few weeks of killing or it would go bad. How was his army to be adequately fed when fighting at such vast distances from home?

To try to solve the problem he offered a prize of about six hundred pounds, a small fortune in those days, for a new method of preserving food. A French chef noted how the bottled milk he bought from a distant farm would stay fresh two or three days longer than the loose milk bought locally. He found it was because the farmer was heating the milk in glass bottles and then sealing them. He assumed, wrongly as it turned out, that the secret of success was the exclusion of air from the bottles.

However he bottled, boiled and sealed both fruits and meat which remained fresh and he won the prize. Millions of sealed glass containers were used to feed the French troops over the next few years.

The British Navy heard about it and also offered a reward. Eventually a prize of five guineas was awarded to Thomas Siddington for his almost identical method of preserving food in glass jars, which were soon used in great quantities by the Admiralty.

But there was one big drawback. Glass bottles were easily broken, a better form of container was required. Round canisters made from thin iron plate were tried. They were easy to make, did not break and having no corners were not even easily dented, but they did have one serious drawback. The acids in the food corroded the container or changed into chemical compounds which either made the food taste bad or in some cases poisoned the food.

A few years later an agent of the Dartford Iron works found a solution, he lined the inside surfaces of the iron plate with a thin coating of tin and ever since these iron containers have been incorrectly known as 'tins'. So successful were these new containers that 'tins' of soup prepared for the Arctic expedition of 1824 were still fresh and edible when opened in 1937, over a hundred years later.

The explorers had also remarked that cans of milk were far preferable to having cows on board, as they didn't have to be fed, or cleaned out and they didn't tumble overboard. Many years after the breakthrough of conserving food Louis Pasteur discovered it was not the exclusion of air that kept the contents fresh but the heating of the contents which killed the harmful bacteria, thereafter this process of sterilisation became known as pasteurisation.

The canisters were filled with food and capped with a lid which had a tiny hole at its centre. It was heated to 270F, the air, gasses and steam escaped, the hole was then sealed with solder and the contents reheated. Even so the contents of an occasional unpunctured tin failed to remain sound and would blow out under the pressure of internal gasses caused by putrification.

To reduce this risk a small quantity of sodium sulphite was added to each tin to absorb any traces of free oxygen and for a few foods chemical preservatives to kill any bacteria not knocked out by heating were added. Which just goes to show that some additives have been around for a very long time.

To return briefly to Napoleon, a possible reason for his downfall at Waterloo was that the diet of the British Army was by then also being supplemented by canned meat and vegetables. Tinned foods were also widely used in the Crimean and Boer Wars where, because the food was in metal containers, the troops nicknamed them 'Iron Rations', a phrase that has stuck as firmly as the labels that were pasted on with almost unremovable glue.

Manufactories set up to produce batches of food in these tin-lined iron-plate canisters became known as 'canning' factories and the canisters 'tin cans'. Meat was precooked under pressure in 'digesters' - now known as 'pressure cookers', but all too often the meat was coarse, stringy and unappetising. On the open market it only sold for half the price of fresh meat and apart from the forces it was only considered fit for consumption by the poor.

To counteract this the meat was ground into small particles and all mixed together, a few 'grains' of salt were added to improve the flavour and from then on it was known as 'corned beef' because the grains of salt were the size of grains of corn.

Around 1860 shipments of canned 'corned beef' started to arrive from Australia and South America. It was called 'Bully beef' from the French word 'boulla' to boil, and not because it was produced from bulls as was widely believed at the time. Indeed the first tin openers of this period were fashioned in the shape of a bull's head. How tins were opened in the fifty years prior to this I have yet to discover.

Fish was another perishable product that could be transported and stored safely in tins. Perhaps the most famous is the sardine tin from Spain and Portugal which requires a special key to open it and is frequently missing or breaks in use!

And have you ever wondered why the sardines are packed in so tightly? It is because the oil which fills the spaces in between is more expensive that the fish, so the greater the space occupied by the fish the less oil is needed and the larger the profit.

Nowadays we tend to think of refrigeration as a modern idea, yet its principles were known in ancient Rome where people stuffed dressed poultry with snow which kept the meat fresh until it thawed. Later a saltpetre mixture was used to chill their table wine making it 'so cold that teeth could hardly endure it', we are told.

From the 1700s no self respecting stately home would be without its 'ice-house' packed with winter ice for storing foods in its cold dank atmosphere.

In the early Victorian days the chilling effect of rapidly evaporating ether used in anaesthetics was also a major factor in the advance of refrigeration - a cheaper commercial alternative was liquid ammonia. The development of these industrial freezers meant that by 1880 shipments of 'chilled' meat could be transported from Australia and sold as 'fresh' meat on the English Market.

In 1912, in America, a certain Clarence Birdseye started experimenting with deep frozen foods after he watched eskimos catch fish in temperatures of minus 50F. They froze stiff immediately they were taken out of the water. Several months later when they were thawed out some of them were still alive!

He also learned to preserve vegetables by placing them in a tub of water and freezing them solid. He set up a frozen food factory in America. People stored his products in ice chests packed with purchased ice or topped up from their own underground ice-house.

Frigidaire introduced the first domestic freezers in 1924. In this country Smedley of Wisbech started freezing asparagus, soft fruits and sliced beans in 1936. Pre-cooked frozen chicken and steaks came onto the market three years later.

The reason why refrigeration works is that it is too cold for the bacteria to breed so food remains uncontaminated.

But back to Napoleon again - the blockade of French ports by the British navy also caused Napoleon another headache and may well have led to one of his best known expressions - 'Not tonight Josephine'.

He could no longer obtain regular supplies of sugar from the sugar canes of the West Indies. It was an important high energy ingredient, not only for sweetening foods but also for preserving fruit. His agriculturalists and scientists got to work extracting sugar from beetroot. Soon new strains with a sugar content of 15% or more were being developed and a completely new farm crop and source of sugar emerged - sugar beet. Within a few years the deficit had been overcome.

Jams and preserves are made by mixing the weight of fruit with from half to equal amounts of sugar, boiling in a brass preserving pan to kill the bacteria, then sealing in sterilised jars made airtight with greaseproof paper tied tightly around the neck with string.

For jellies the extracted liquid is mixed with from a third to a half its weight of sugar then boiled and sealed as before. Fruit, either whole or sliced, can also be boiled in a sugar solution. When removed and dried the sugar crystallises to produce 'candied' or 'crystallised' fruits. My granny used to love to receive a box of these at Christmas time.

Fruit and vegetables could also be boiled and after the addition of salt and sugar, sealed into wide-necked glass storage bottles with a rubber sealing ring and a screw cap, called 'Kilner jars'. We used to have rows of them along our pantry and cellar shelves. They contained all the surplus fruit and vegetables from the garden and provided us with tasty vegetables, tarts and pies throughout the whole of winter.

Yes, Napoleon once called us a nation of shopkeepers yet even he could never have imagined that two hundred years on our shops would be stocked full of food preserved by methods he inaugurated and developed out of necessity during the rise and fall of his empire.

177 February Wife Selling
'SORRY DEAR, YOU'LL HAVE TO BE SOLD'

'HEAR ye; Hear ye; Hear ye; Wives for sale; wives for sale. At two of the clock at the Market Cross. Come and see, come and buy. Hear ye; Hear ye; Hear ye.'

The origins of many of our older customs of courtship and marriage are well documented, but what isn't usually mentioned is what happened to couples who, after marriage, found they just couldn't get on together.

How could they separate? Before the Matrimonial Clauses Act of 1857 there were two methods, one for the rich and one for the poor.

In order to obtain an official dissolution of a marriage, it had to go through lengthy legal channels and a private Act of Parliament, both costly and cumbersome and restricted to the rich.

Rules drawn up after the Reformation meant that the church only recognised divorce, 'the removal of the wife from the table and the bed', for very few reasons. The most useful of which, as far as the poor were concerned, was that if a partner had not been heard of for seven years they could be presumed dead and the survivor was then allowed to remarry.

This sometimes led to complications such as when soldiers were fighting distant wars, people were press-ganged into serving on ships or when a young married chap set off to seek his fortune and it took a lot longer than he had expected. He eventually returned home only to find his wife had remarried and probably had a family

Of course some couples took advantage of the ruling and by mutual agreement one of them deliberately 'disappeared' leaving them both free to remarry in future. But for about two hundred years there was a much quicker and cheaper way of separating. It was for a husband to SELL his wife.

Although it was not 'officially' recognised, it was a way open to less wealthy members of society and was regarded by the vast majority as legitimate providing certain rules were obeyed. First the wife had to agree to be sold. Second the sale had to be in a public place and well publicised. Third, the wife was to be conducted from her home to the place of sale with a halter around her neck. At the conclusion of the sale and the completion of the payment the new owner was to lead her by the same halter and was not to remove it until she was safely settled in her new home - and had herself closed the door behind her.

Fourth, no wife could be sold for less than one shilling. Her original husband was now free to marry again.

As a result of these rules wives were usually offered for sale on market days, during the annual fair (as in the opening chapter of Thomas Hardy's Mayor of Casterbridge), or in public houses. The forthcoming sale was advertised in the local paper, generally after the cattle advertisements in the market columns. A considerable number were reported in The Times broadsheets and the Town Crier also informed people.

According to ancient lore a wife was considered 'chattel' from the Anglo-Saxon custom of a groom paying a 'purchase' price to the bride's father at the church door to compensate for the loss of his daughter's services. On the morning following the wedding, the 'husband' would give his bride a gift as a token that he was satisfied with his purchase, after which he could not return her. As with the sale of animals the payment of money and the transfer of the halter was believed to give complete legality to the sale of the wife.

The auctioneer entered the sales into the Market Record Book. The usual fee was one penny, but when Mr Hilton sold his wife at Brighton Market in May 1826 he was charged one shilling. On challenging this exorbitant amount the clerk quoted from the market rules concerning animal sales that 'Any article not enumerated in these Bye-Laws pays one shilling.' Obviously the sale of wives was not included in his book of rules.

On 7th April 1832, a Cumberland farmer, Joseph Thomson, who had been unhappily married for three years took his wife Mary to Carlisle market with a STRAW halter around her neck and offered her for sale to the 'highest and fairest bidder'

A flier describing her bad points claiming that 'I took her for my comfort and the good of my house, but she became my tormentor, a domestic curse, a bosom serpent, a night invasion and a daily devil'. He then shrewdly listed her good points which were: 'She can sing, read novels, plait her frills and caps, milk cows, make butter and scold the maid, and I offer her at the price of fifty shillings.'

She was eventually sold to Henry Mears who bought her for £1 and a Newfoundland dog. It was reported afterwards that 'Neither the dog nor the woman gave so much as a backward glance at their previous masters as they parted company'.

There are many such instances where a system of barter was used instead of, or in addition to a payment of money. In 1831, at Bolton, Lancs, a wife was sold for three shillings and sixpence and a gallon of ale, whilst in Hereford in 1802 a butcher sold his wife for twenty four shillings and a bowl of punch. One farmer from Suffolk exchanged his wife for a bullock which he later sold for six guineas. The wife however did not find her new partner to her liking and after a while she returned to her former husband.

Another Suffolk farmer was so glad to be rid of his wife that from the five guineas he received from the sale, he gave her a guinea to buy a new gown and had a peal of bells rung from Stowmarket church in celebration.

'If at first you don't succeed try, try again' for according to a newspaper report one wife offered for sale at a Bath market in August 1833 was 'dashingly attired' and her halter was covered in silk but the bidding only reached five shillings whereupon the husband took her home again. It was in fact the second time he had failed. She had previously been offered at Lansdown Fair where she had been purchased for half a crown when it was discovered that the buyer was already married.

A somewhat similar situation was reported in the Chester Chronicle of 1799. A man named Twig bought TWO wives at Macclesfield market. He paid half a crown for the one, and a shilling for the other even through he was already married and living with his wife. However no action seems to have been taken against him.

Until 1858 adultery was not considered a reason for divorce, but by selling a wife at auction a husband could dispose of the liabilities of his wife and in some case also her children. There was often prior collusion between the parties concerned. At Chapel en le Frith, a wife, child and furniture were sold for eleven shillings at the market cross.

Of course, 'selling' a wife was not recognised by everybody. A magistrate in Yorkshire imposed a month's hard labour on Joshua Jackson for doing just that. It almost caused a riot among the local people. Much more fortunate was Hugh Pritchard who sold his wife at Manchester - he only suffered a reprimand from the magistrate.

A parson in Devon who refused to register a 'purchased' wife's death, was neatly out-manouvered when the husband laid her to rest in the churchyard of the adjoining parish where the parson had no such qualms.

In case you are thinking that it was mainly ageing, unattractive wives that were being sold by old men long in the tooth who wished to replace them with a younger version I'm sorry to disappoint you for the opposite was the reality.

In almost every instance of 'selling' the couple had lived together for less than twelve years. One young man even parted with his bride after a few days. She was sold to a comrade for five guineas. He paid one guinea down and took her on a month's trial! Was this an early example of 'buy now and pay later' or was it 'pay as you learn'?

The last recorded sales I have read about were in Devon and Monmouth in1928 and at Swaffham Bulbeck in Cambridgeshire in 1933.

And of course there is the story of the hen-pecked husband who took his domineering wife to market and sold her for half a crown. He bought another at auction for two shillings making himself a profit of sixpence on the deal. However when he got her home she turned out to be 'TWICE AS BAD' as the one he had sold. Certainly a case of 'CAVEAT EMPTOR' - 'BUYER BEWARE'.

So for any unattached ladies reading this who are wondering whether to pop the question this Leap Year, it may be worth considering if you have already passed your SELL BY date!

178 March Farmhouses
'THE CHANGING FACE OF THE FARM HOUSE'

Although almost every parish has several farmhouses, I have yet to discover two that are the same. The differences between them depend on when they were built, where they were built and what type of farming was being practised at the time.

As a rule the oldest ones are to be found at the heart of the village, on either side of the roads that pass through, the reason being that in bygone days people clustered together in the centre for safety. From these central farms livestock was taken daily to the outskirts of the village to the commons, the communal grazing grounds further afield.

During the two main development periods of Elizabeth I's time and the Agrarian Revolution of the mid 1700s, many of these common lands were enclosed to make new farms and new farms needed new farmhouses.

Until the Industrial Revolution farming was the hub around which village life revolved, everyone depended on it. The landlord and his estate workers relied for their very existence on the rent paid by the farmers, and it was agriculture, not the estates, which were by far the biggest employers of labour in the countryside.

The Yeoman farmers of England were so called because in times of war they were the bowmen of England whose bows were made of yew so they were in fact 'yewmen''. As a result of an outdoor life of strenuous work they were a breed of hardy, energetic, vigorous men, full of common sense gained by years of practical experience.

By their own hard graft they became prosperous. Any that were frail or failed, fell by the wayside and their land was taken over by other farmers who were quite literally more competent in the field.

When the primitive, earth-floored hovels in which farmers then lived burned down or started to collapse through lack of foundations, they were replaced by farmhouses that stood solid and four square and were purpose-built for the needs of the farming methods at that time. Hard won fortunes were not frittered away on frills and fashion, farmhouses were designed as working homes not for leisure or pleasure.

They were built to last by local people using local materials that blended in with the local landscape and probably of equal importance, the money spent stayed within the community to enrich the lives of others. As an example, a wooden framed farmhouse required the timber from about three hundred oak trees. Building it gave employment to foresters, woodsmen, sawyers, carters and carpenters as well as blacksmiths who made the tools and fashioned the ironwork.

The framework was constructed from green, unseasoned wood and assembled like a jig-saw flat on the ground. The joints were marked, it was all taken to pieces, then reassembled in its upright position. The mortices and tenons were held in place with tapered oak pegs.

The spaces between the woodwork were filled with wattles - woven willow-work - and covered with daub - a mixture of clay, lime, straw, hair and manure.

Brick chimney breasts were added and the roof thatched. Again, local lads dug out the clay from the marl pits which later became farmyard ponds, the village brickmaker moulded and fired the clay, others laid the bricks and the local thatcher put the reeds on the steep, sixty degree angled roof which helped to prevent rainwater penetrating the thatch.

Deep carved bargeboards were added at the gable ends to stop the wind lifting the edges of the thatch and long handled rakes with curved, barbed iron ends were hung under the eaves to remove the thatch rapidly in case of fire. In some towns thatch was banned because of the risk of such conflagrations.

As the green woodwork slowly seasoned it shrank, twisted, turned and distorted which is why old timber houses have sloping floors, doors and walls which lean at all sorts of unusual angles and also explains how Chesterfield church came to have its famous twisted spire. Yet for all their faults many of these locally built wooden farmhouses have survived for over four hundred years and have become recognised as buildings of outstanding architectural merit today.

The farmhouse was the pivotal point of the life of the farm, and the work that was done both within and without was carried out in harmony and in sympathy with the seasons.

Stock buildings were usually arranged on the northern side so that the prevailing south west winds would blow most of the foul smells away. If the farm had cows a dairy was built next to the larder on the north side of the farmhouse as an extension. It was often sunken down two or three steps to keep it even cooler. To avoid paying window tax the word 'dairy' was painted over the horizontal louvres that let in the light and air.

Most farmhouses were serviced by two staircases, which derived from the old 'Hall' where the central portion was open to the roof. This proved a blessing in disguise, for the farmer and his family used the staircase which led to the bedrooms that overlooked the farmyard, whilst the many unmarried workers who 'lived in' used the other. These were often orphans or illegitimate children who were 'farmed out' by the churchwardens or Parish overseer.

Girls worked in the kitchen, scullery and dairy. They milked the cows and saw to the chickens. Lads helped with the fieldwork, the feeding and cleaning out of the stock. They were all part of the farmer's extended family, they worked together, lived under the same roof and had their meals together.

Three meals a day meant that the kitchen was always a hive of activity. The stock pot, hanging from the adjustable swinging chimney crane; the heavy iron kettle with its 'idleback' lever that allowed it to be poured without lifting and the oven beside the log fire in the large inglenook, none of them ever had a chance to go cold or rusty.

Freshly baked bread was stored on ceiling racks for four days before being eaten, if eaten fresh some farmhands would eat far too much too quickly and might suffer from acute indigestion as a result. Older bread was also better for toasting. The fireplace was large enough for everyone to sit around on winter evenings.

Up the spacious chimney were hooks to hang bacons and hams for smoking. Only oak or ash was burned then, as pine smoke would taint the meat. Hooks were also to be found along every beam and from them hung the flitches and joints, bunches of herbs and baskets of vegetables that were required to feed the ever-hungry occupants.

The kitchen door was the most used one in the house, the front door was only opened on special occasions such as christenings, weddings, funerals or when the vicar called. It was always very difficult to open, its bolts were rusty with disuse, its hinges creaked and groaned and the woodwork was warped.

To provide extra storage space the area of the farmhouse was increased by the excavation of cellars. There, on stone slabs covered with a layer of clean wheat straw were kept the autumnal benevolence of apples, pears, beetroots, turnips, potatoes and freshly killed meat, barrels of beer and bottles of wine.

At the top of the house were the attics, originally a long gallery where the loom clacked and cloth was woven. When it became cheaper to buy clothing and garments rather than make them on the farm, the attics became dormitories for either the boys or the girls who lived in - sometimes for both - unofficially of course!

Another essential extension was the wash-house. Here the staff could clean themselves up before coming in for meals or for bed. But its most important function was the weekly wash. Soft water, channelled along lead-lined V-shaped wooden gutters at the eaves and stored in old wine butts by the back door was put into the 'copper' with a fire underneath. The clothes of all the household were boiled and bashed, wrung and rinsed then pegged outside on the line to dry in fine weather, or hung from wooden racks called 'ceiling maidens' in the kitchen in wet weather.

Just outside the kitchen door, occasionally even inside, was the well where essential buckets of drinking water could be drawn up. Later the well was capped and a pump with its long counter-weighted handle raised the water instead.

Many windows were bricked up to reduce the window tax, while the remainder almost permanently open to 'air' the house, reduce condensation and prevent mould forming on the walls. In towns the contents of the bedroom chamber pots were emptied through the upstairs windows into the street but farmhouses had a much more hygienic method. A small bedroom cupboard hid a funnel that ran through the wall and down into the farmyard manure heap.

Almost every cupboard, panel, door and floor had a mouse or rat hole in one corner or another where rodents had nibbled through in search of food and shelter.

Although hill farmers eked out a meagre subsistence which barely alternated between survival and starvation, they managed to build stout stone farmhouses with extremely thick walls to keep out the rain, wind and cold.

In northern areas the farmer, his family, animals and corn were all housed under one roof in what was called a 'longhouse' or 'laithe'. Each helped to keep the other warm. The low boards which held the grain on the threshing floor, and had to be stepped over in passing, gave the origin to our 'threshhold'.

When expansion was required nothern farmers extended their farmhouses lengthwise, remaining at one room width. Those further south built a new brick facade onto the front or extended the rear, making it two rooms deep, a feature which has continued ever since.

The passing years have seen many changes. When the small farmhouses that once straddled the village street became redundant, they were transformed into attractive country cottages by those wealthy enough to be able to move into the countryside. In place of the wood burning fire in the inglenook now stands a multi-purpose fuel stove that not only cooks and boils the kettle but supplies hot water to heat the radiators to warm the whole house instead of just the kitchen. Windows once wide open are now double glazed and permanently shut for fear of intruders.

Washing no longer dries on the line or hangs from the ceiling maidens, moisture is extracted mechanically by modern tumble driers instead. The hooks on the beams and the stone slabs in the cellar are bare, all the food required for months ahead can be stored far more easily in fridges and freezers.

Instead of a battalion of farmworkers 'living in', the farmer's wife takes in paying guests on a 'bed and breakfast' basis to occupy the vacant rooms and since the bedrooms are equipped with full ensuite facilities, there is no longer any need for the funnel discreetly hidden in the cupboard!

The chatter, comments and laughter of the household staff and workers crammed around the fireside at night has been replaced by the monotonous drone of the radio or the television set blaring away almost unnoticed in the comer.

Yet the farmhouse is still the focal point of life on the farm; the kitchen door the most frequently used and the front door still refusing to open on those rare occasions it is asked - for a wedding, a funeral, or when the vicar comes to call.

179 April May Day customs
'ANCIENT CEREMONIES TO WELCOME THE NEW SEASON'

'WINTER IS DEAD, SUMMER HAS COME'

That is what people once shouted at dawn on the first of May. To try to understand how important the day was to them and what they did we have to seek clues from our present picturesque May Day ceremonies. You will see items emerge to form a pattern of belief that was completely natural to them, but leaves many modern folk aghast with horror.

Let me set the current scene. The children from the local school parade two by two through the village. The girls are dressed in white and wear flowers in their hair, the boys look unusually smart in their best clothes. The procession is led by the prettiest girl, the 'Queen of the May', closely attended by an unidentifiable person swathed in interwoven green boughs.

On reaching the maypole each child takes hold of a coloured ribbon, boys and girls dance in opposite directions, criss-crossing one another alternately which makes an attractive plait down the stem of the maypole.

At the end of their performance the audience of admiring parents and onlookers applaud and the children leave to tuck in to some well-earned refreshments, they then play games for the rest of the day.

Meanwhile Morris dancers hold the crowd's attention with their complicated steps, jingling bells, clapping of hands, slapping of sticks and severing with swords.

During the day, to the thrill and encouragement of the audience - one or two young men a little the worse for wear, having already had too much to drink, attempt to climb the maypole and touch the top, much to the consternation of the stewards who wonder if their insurance is sufficient to cover such accidents. One reaches the top without incident except a great roar of approval from the crowd.

As daylight diminishes a bonfire is lit and a barbecue serves hot dogs and hamburgers. Late in the evening the young lads jump over the glowing embers for a dare. Most make it, one doesn't and has a brown scorch hole in his trousers to add to his embarrasment. The night grows cold and everyone returns home. The May Day holiday is over for another year.

Now to the scene as it was, one, two, three thousand years ago or more.

Our ancestors were surrounded on all sides by forests, there were trees everywhere, dark, dense and spooky. People believed that every living thing contained a spirit and being forest dwellers the one they feared and respected most was the tree spirit, which is why even today we 'touch wood', if we are boastful about our health or wealth.

People also pondered on the divisions between life and death, summer and winter, the real and the spirit world. To them each had a definite beginning and a definite end. The 1st November and the 1st of May were the only two days in the year when all these items intermingled.

Tree spirits were believed to be endowed with the power to make the rain to fall, the sun to shine, food and herds to multiply and women to become pregnant. Which is why, on the Eve of May Day, the sturdy lads and buxom lasses would spend the night in the nearby woods.

There, among other activities that provided an increase in the population within the year, they found time to cut down a large straight tree, lop off all but the topmost branches and decorate it with garlands of greenery and woodland flowers. They made garlands for themselves and nosegays for the village oxen that dragged the great tree - the May Pole - the symbol of Summer, back to the village an hour or so before dawn.

It was raised upright, next to the blazing bonfire at the very centre of the area where they regularly worshipped, on the sacred barrow tumuli, hilltop, grove or within their stone circle.

Then their gaze was diverted to the beckoning line of fiery beacons that blazed on the many hilltops that stretched away into the distance as they waited for the sun to rise. It did, as if by magic, exactly at the point on the horizon indicated by the line of fires, it was the only day of the year on which it could happen.

They shouted and blew on their horns to welcome the arrival of the summer. At that very moment the elected 'King' of the tribe was ceremoniously sacrificed at the base of the maypole as a sign that the Winter was Dead and as an appeasement to the tree-gods who would now ensure the fertility of man and beast for the coming year. The body of the executed 'King' was covered with green branches from oak and hawthorn, their religious trees. Whilst unnoticed a 'living' young man slipped inside a prepared framework totally enclosed with intertwining oak and hawthorn branches and took his place beside the Queen of the May.

The dead 'King' of winter had been transformed into the 'Green Man' of Summer, vegetation had returned to clothe the earth after its six months of hibernation.

From medieval times and throughout the middle ages the legendary figure of Robin Hood dressed in his costume of Sherwood Green, replaced the original 'Green Man', and Maid Marian took over from the Queen of the May, which is how these two characters and others of their merry men came to be part of the procession. A stained glass window in the parish of Betley, Staffordshire depicts them and individual morris dancers.

It was because of the sacrifice of the 'King' that most of our church fetes today only have a Rose Queen and her attendants, there is seldom a king, yet curiously enough the 'King', in the form of the 'Green Man', can be found carved in stone in many of our churches, his head encircled in oak or hawthorn branches which eminate from his mouth. St Mary's, Nantwich has some famous examples.

The withdrawal to the woods on the eve of May was the start of the 'pairing off' process for the eligible lads and lasses, with the intention of wedlock if they both proved fertile. It was the forerunner of the 'holdfast' or 'handfast' custom during which they lived together for a trial period of a year and a day and only married if they conceived.

The maypole represented the tree spirit which is why it was so honoured. When trees became scarcer the same pole was used for several years. To renew its vigour it was retopped each May Day by splicing on a head of new green branches.

The climbing of the Maypole to perform this task was considered a great honour - as it was, if anyone else could climb it and bring down a leaf from the crown. A development of this was climbing the greasy pole for the reward of a prize pig.

The Morris Men with their moorish, military style steps often had blackened faces to hide their identity. They performed the 'Long' dance in procession and the 'Cross' dance at stopping places. The clattering of their clogs and the tinkling of their bells were specifically to drive off evil spirits.

Onlookers were often rewarded with a morsel of cake carried on a sword. But male members had to beware if the cake contained a 'bean' secreted in it, that person became the 'bean king' and organised the games to be played. In fact, he had a beanfeast or a 'beano' while it lasted, but at dawn on the next first of May the 'bean king' became a 'has been'.

This is why at the end of the sword dance the dancers interlock their swords around the 'head' of their leader and lift the still interlocked swords on high in joyful acclaim. This now innocent end of the dance ritual depicts the decapitating of the 'king' and his severed head held high to show the world 'Winter is dead, summer is come'.

The weaving movements of the dancers around the maypole, later using coloured ribbons, was believed to bind the sun to the earth and copied the patterns of the progress of the stars and planets through the heavens. The whirling and twirling gave the participants a dizziness which linked them to the landscape, quite literally if they fell down exhausted. They gave their energy to the earth and in due course would receive their energy from it again.

They also danced around the district in a snake like fashion following the paths of the local maze and the Nine Man Morris patterns cut into the turf.

During the day, before being set free to graze, the oxen and other cattle were walked through the smoke of the still smouldering fire to ward off evil and ensure a plentiful future supply of milk. Burning brands were also taken to every field of the parish to cleanse them from any evil spirits left over and lurking from winter. The lads and lasses would pair up again and jump over the hot ashes to ensure their fertility - it must have worked or we wouldn't be here to tell the tale today!

So as you see our present ceremonies do give us quite a few glimpses into what May Day really meant to our ancestors. I hope my rather explicit explanations do not spoil your enjoyment of May day - the first day of summer.

180 May Smell
'MAKING SENSE IN A WORLD OF SMELLS'

WE all have one, we use it every minute of the day and night, it never walks but it occasionally runs. After over-indulgence it can become as red as a beetroot, and when we were young and wanted to find somewhere, we were told to follow it. If you've guessed what it is, you've won - by a nose!

As the receptor of one of our five senses we seldom give it a second thought, until we have a bad cold in the head, then, because we cannot smell, our food doesn't taste the same.

The main function of our nose is to warm, filter and moisten the air that enters our lungs. On its way the air passes over receptors that notice minute variations in chemical compounds and send a message to the brain which identifies the smell.

We are able to distinguish some smells even when they are diluted to one part in fifty thousand million parts of air.

Yet that is only a fraction of the sensitivity some animals have. A dog's sense of smell is about a hundred times greater than ours. Human smell sensors cover an area about the size of a postage stamp whereas that of a dog will cover a mansize pocket handkerchief. That is why they are so good for tracking.

When we walk we give off a natural cloud of invisible scent particles roughly the same size and shape as our body. They slowly fall to earth, sink into the ground and are eventually lost.

A normal dog can follow this scent several hours later, a bloodhound for up to a week. Occasionally the dog may pause to paw the ground because the scent has passed below the surface and is stronger underneath. It is this amazing sense of smell that gives them the ability to sniff out drugs and, in France, truffles, though for this purpose pigs are even more sensitive, they can home in on a buried truffle from fifty yards away. Almost all animals utilise their powers of smell more than we do, they use them for communication, guidance, and for finding food.

Every breed of animal has a different smell and each animal within that species will have a variation of communal smell according to its health, status and breeding condition. To give you a few practical examples: foxes and dogs urinate on buried bones and carcasses as proof of identity to assist in finding them later. Squirrels are guided to their winter stores by the smell of their saliva.

In my herd a cow would be rejected and sent to Coventry by the rest long before I noticed anything was wrong with her. When my bull ran with the cows he would sniff each one as she urinated to tell her breeding condition. If she was coming into season and ripe for mating his nose would wrinkle and make his bull ring stand upright, a posture called Flehmen caused by the excitement of the 'organ of Jacobson' - a small bone encased structure just above the palate which is very sensitive to sexual odours.

He would also frequently emit a scent almost indistinguishable to my nose from the smell of 'Brut' soap my wife used to buy me. I wonder if she was trying to tell me something?

One cowman I knew claimed he could smell when a cow was ready for service and he was right nearly every time. I never gained that sensitivity of smell but there are a great many distinctive farming smells such as foot rot, acetonemia, calving and scouring that farmers and vets can identify as soon as they enter the cow-shed.

In bygone days when milk was collected and transported in churns it was accepted or rejected at the dairy by the 'nose' of the weighing inspector who sniffed the contents when he lifted the lid before he tipped it. If he was in any doubt a sample was sent to the laboratory for analysis. So accurate was his diagnosis that the churn of milk was usually returned to the farmer with a rejection slip. Fortunately for me it seldom happened.

Shepherds know that the smell of a ram helps to induce fertility into their sheep. After lambing a very strong scent bond is established between the ewe and her lambs when she cleans its birth fluid and thereafter she recognises it by smell. In order to introduce an orphan lamb the ancient practice was to cover it with the same birth fluid or the skin of her own lamb if it had died in which case she might accept it as her own.

Most animals consume their afterbirth to destroy the evidence to prowling predators. Young rats and mice have a tendancy to wander from the nest, to overcome this the mother produces a strong maternal odour that keeps them under her strict control until they mature. The scent bond keeps colonies together. Strangers have a different smell and can be recognised. This is how bees, whose hives are clustered together, identify which hive is theirs. If they attempt to enter another hive their smell will alert the 'soldier' bees on guard and they will be expelled. When bees or wasps sting they also release a tiny drop of scent (pheromone) on the spot so that others can home in and sting the same target, which gives credence to the cartoon of a person being chased by an angry swarm.

Drones are attracted to the Virgin Queen by her scent, which also induces them to mate. So much so that she is often mobbed by a large number flying in from several hundred yards away. Every successful drone thereafter carries a bit of the Queen's scent and in turn is chased by others.

Smell is very important in evading danger. Any hunter will tell you animals can smell a human a mile or more away which is why it is so important to keep 'downwind' of your quarry.

When our bitch was in season we had dogs 'visiting' her from a considerable distance away. Size is not a factor for it has been proved that an Emperor moth can identify the pheromone of a female anxious to mate from three miles away providing he is 'downwind'. He will usually reach her within half an hour - he 'homes in' on her at six miles per hour.

Flowers give off scent to encourage insects to pollinate them, but the crafty cabbage white butterfly seeks out the smell from nasturtium and cabbage leaves on which to lay her eggs and feed her caterpillars. Other butterflies and moths also find their habitat by the smell of their respective plants and trees. The Sexton beetle discovers its recently deceased prey by smell and very soon a dozen or more will have gathered to bury the carcass beneath the ground, whilst a polar bear is said to be able to smell a dead seal from up to twelve miles away.

But perhaps the foulest smell that nature produces is not the stench of putrifaction from decomposing corpses but the foul aroma given off by the stinkhorn fungus - to attract blow flies.

Animals cannot put up notice boards saying 'Private Property - Keep Out', so males advertise their boundaries in a much more subtle manner - by smell. At certain vantage points along the outer limits of their normal range male members squirt their urine or leave their faeces as a signal to other males that although they can pass through, the territory is already taken.

As the scent markers can often last for many weeks it is much less arduous for the animal than constantly patrolling the area. As a rule the males only aggressively defend a much smaller central area.

These boundary markings serve to give the defender a psychological advantage over any male intruder. The scent markers however have exactly the opposite effect on females, they are encouraged and attracted into the area, sexually aroused and spurred on to mate by the smell. Stags do this in the rutting season. The strongest scent gathers the largest harem of receptive females.

So if in future you see a dog lifting his leg against a lamp post he is only doing what nature intended and leaving his mating mark. Don't turn your nose up at it, which leads me back to noses and nicely on to the fact that the original 'Nosey Parker' was an Archbishop of Canterbury during the reign of Queen Elizabeth I, and also that my biology teacher at school said we were all perfectly designed to sniff out any problem in life, for if we had been fashioned with our noses pointing upwards we might have smelt a bit more but if we ever went out in a thunderstorm we would probably drown.

181 June Weeds
'HI- HOE, HI- HOE, IT'S OFF TO WORK WE GO'

As every farmer and gardener will tell you, whether it is 'flaming' or 'bursting out all over' JUNE is the month when the weeds REALLY grow. They emerge as if by magic in any patch of fertile soil that remains undisturbed for long enough to allow them to germinate. Gardeners deal with them by pulling them out, hoeing them off, covering the area with mulch or carpeting it with discarded floor coverings.

Nowadays farmers generally try to control weeds with expensive herbicide sprays, their effectiveness can easily be gauged by any strips that are missed, the flora of which soon becomes the talk of the neighbourhood.

It is only a few years ago that the whole economy of the countryside, the winter welfare of the parish and the prosperity of farms was determined by the control of weeds in the crops. The main thing was to try to destroy them when they were small. In corn crops, providing the weather was warm and the soil was dry, light harrows were dragged through.

Their weight was just sufficient to disturb the weeds but not enough to up-root the corn. It gave the crop about a two week advantage over the weeds and in most years was sufficient to smother any future re-growth of weeds.

In some areas it was the custom to turn pigs loose into the growing corn if it was infested with poppies. They so enjoyed the seedlings that they left the corn alone. Later in the season the farmer, his staff and local helpers walked through the maturing corn pulling out rogue plants and weeds, the most common of which were redshank, yellow charlock and wild oats, (every farmer was said to sow some, especially when young).

We all wore a sack apron around our waist into which the weeds were put. They were dumped in piles in the ditch or hedge when we reached the headland. We walked the rows of corn until the field had been completed. On dry days it was a happy communal task, but on cold, wet days or after a shower the whole of the lower half of your body soon became saturated and heavy with clinging clay or soil from the roots of the weeds.

Thistles were cut off just below soil level with a sharp two inch metal blade called a 'spudder'. When corn was harvested by hand the farmer had to provide his workers with gloves if the crop was heavily infested with thistles.

Where thistles were the scourge of meadowland they were scythed. I always found this a most depressing job because it was done on damp days when we couldn't get on with our haymaking - because of a depression! Yes, our moods have a lot in common with our weather!

For heavily infested areas an OLD grass mower was used, because not having a full cut and occasionally running empty or going through molehills it would shake the machine to smithereens, soon wear down the bearing surfaces or break rivets, sections, or bar of the cutting knife. There are several types of thistles, tame rabbits and cage birds love the soft, milky 'sow' thistles, cows will eat some of the common ones when cut, but I have never known anything tackle the beautiful 'scotch' thistle except butterfly caterpillars.

The worst thistle of all is the deadly, spiny 'Boar' thistle, the most effective way of dealing with it is to cut it off below ground level with a spade and carefully dump it out of harms way for it takes a long time firking thistle thorns out of your fingers with a needle until they fester. A well known and true saying about controlling thistles is: 'cut them in May and they'll grow back again next day, cut them in June and you've cut them too soon, cut them in July and they're sure to die'.

It was also a tricky job cutting bogs of mature nettles, their long stems were just as likely to fall forward onto your hands and arms as fall sideways with the sweep of the scythe. When we had free-range hens roaming the farmyard we often found a clutch of eggs being incubated in the nettles. We left them until the proud mother brought her fluffy yellow chicks home to the farm for the approval of the cockerel and the satisfaction of us all before cutting that particular clump.

Docks were removed with a special forked tool, which had a fulcrum underneath, an enlarged version of the gardeners dandelion or daisy lifter. The fork was pushed under the

fanged roots and levered upwards, hopefully pulling the roots out intact because any pieces that broke off would mature into full size docks the following year.

When I came to this farm nearly forty years ago it took me most of my spare time every June eliminating docks, nettles and thistles but by sheer perseverance I got it down to a couple of days without the use of sprays.

'Roots' came into cultivation around the 1800s. The varieties were ordinary turnips used both for the household eating and feeding sheep. The winter hardy turnip from Sweden we now call a 'SWEDE', and mangels, mangolds or mangelwurzles, depending on district and dialect. These football size, succulent juicy red or orange globes contained a lot of water. They were a very useful supplement for winter feeding of cattle before the introduction of water bowls. Considerably later came the commercial growing of sugar beet. During the first twenty years of my farming career I grew all of these varieties. The method of controlling weeds in them was, the seeds were sown in continuous rows in wide drills about two feet apart, sometimes on ridges. On a fine day, as soon as the seedlings had emerged the space between the rows was disturbed by horse hoeing,

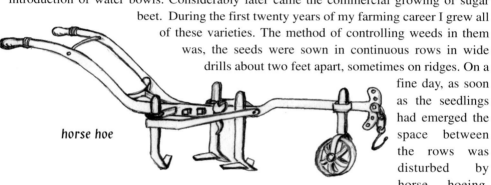

horse hoe

scarifying or scuffling. They were all closely related, two horizontal hoes or bars angled slightly backwards were set as close as possible to the seedlings, in the space in between was a horizontal 'ducks foot' hoe, all were adjustable and bolted onto a rigid 'V' shaped frame. Sometimes the seedlings were so small you needed glasses to see them, but within a day or two they were growing apace, but so also were the weeds!

Wet weather at this stage meant a lot of work later on for even disturbed weeds re-rooted and grew again smothering the crop. The continuous rows of seedlings were then thinned by hand hoe, leaving the most forward and best 'cock' plants about 8 inches (20 cm) apart. The rhythm was push, pull, push, pull with the seven inch hoe at a slow sideways walking pace. 'Swan necked' hoes were perfect as the pointed tip of the hoe could separate two close growing seedlings with only a slight twist of the wrist. The best blades were blacksmith made and fashioned from a thin scythe blade. Factory ones were thick and needed sharpening frequently to cut the weeds. The rubbish, unwanted seedlings and weeds were hoed into the centre between the rows or base of the ridges, where if it was sunny they would soon wither and die. If not they would be disturbed by horse hoeing about every two weeks to stop them growing again. 'Singleing' was usually set on a piece work basis. Each worker was allocated twenty rows in turn across the field and marked with a stick. Payment was 'sixpence per score' - that was for every twenty yards hoed. It was no use hurrying and scampering your work to get it over quicker, leave weeds or double plants because the agreement was that all work had to be gone over again two weeks later and pass the farmer's critical eye before payment was forthcoming.

Everyone liked piece work, it was a welcome chance to earn extra money. A gang of trusty men and women from the local town regularly helped us. They put in a couple of hours before they went to work in the morning and about four hours in the evening, more if there was enough light from the moon.

Singleing had to be done within about three weeks of emergence or the plants would be too big and the yield would suffer, it was a hectic race against time. The hoeing season was a back aching time until you got used to it. The first week was the worst , the remedy was once your back was bent, keep it bent don't straighten up! But on good days it was a very happy and interesting job, chatting away to hoers on their neighbouring sections. It was always exciting to find pewits', plovers' or skylarks' nests and mark them with a stick so that the horse hoes would not disturb them until the fledglings had flown - or run away - for trying to pick up a peewit chick was like picking up quicksilver, with the parent birds feigning injury or sweeping low in alarm.

There were many unexpected treats, the dawn chorus and the lesser evening songs, old rooks teaching the young how to catch grubs or the sight of a sly, old fox slinking along the hedgerow, seeking a supper from a nest of incubating pheasant or partridge eggs.

Sometimes we anxiously worked away as anvil shaped storm clouds gathered overhead and ran to shelter under a holly or hawthorn bush as the hailstones bounced on the field followed by a blast of sweeping torrential rain which carved tunnels in the soft soil and sometimes washed the plants away. It was slow, soggy, sticky hoeing for the next hour or two with frequent stops to wipe mud from the hoe blade between finger and thumb or knocking the back of the swan neck on a stone to dislodge it. Sometimes hares, rabbits or slugs would destroy several yards of plants leaving the leaves hanging on by a thread-like thin strand of stem. Rather than leave the area to waste we usually re-seed any larger patches with a gaping drill. After the second hoeing we usually walked through the crop on day work a month or so later to take out any persistent weeds.

We also did this along the potato ridges - 'fat hen' (also called 'Good King Henry', an edible brassica) was usually the worst weed to eliminate. The hoeing I remember best was just before I got married one June. My father-in-law said he wanted his sugar beet singled before he would hand over his daughter. We finished the field the night before the wedding!! At the end of the day there was always the satisfaction of seeing clean crops and clean fields that would have vast, good yields. The season of long working days and short nights also had its advantages, you slept sound - almost as soon as your head touched the pillow - even on honeymoon.

182 July   Village Greens
'CENTRAL TO VILLAGE LIFE'

An important feature of Anglo-Saxon settlements was the Village Green, almost every village had one.

But why was this open space left at the centre of the village? What were its uses and why have so many disappeared that today comparative few are left? There is a great deal of controversy over their original function. In many cases it is difficult to differentiate between 'village greens' and 'commons' for both seem inextricably interlinked.

No two are ever the same. They vary in size from a small plot to an area of up to a hundred acres. Some villages only had one, others had several, in one case nine and in another, ten scattered around the parish.

The shape of the 'green' does not fall into any regular pattern either. Although the majority are triangular, some are square, whilst others are composed of one or two long, narrow, irregular shaped strips.

One fact that is common to most is that the houses, formerly huts and hovels, mainly face towards the green.

It has been suggested that greens were for defence when raiding parties were abroad. The villagers would confine their animals on the green surrounded by the protection of their homes, but as only a few examples occur where border raids were common place, the more generally accepted theory is that livestock sheltered on the green overnight to protect them from predators such as wolves and foxes.

The triangular village green is thought to have evolved from ancient farming practices when every villager cultivated strips of land in each of the three arable fields of the village, on a rotational basis of two years cropping and one year fallow. The three fields would be situated near the centre of the parish and provide a reason for the three sides of the village green. They were the common property of all the inhabitants for grazing - and a multitude of other uses.

In 1376 Edward III decreed that to maintain law and order, every village had to erect a set of stocks in which minor offenders could be placed to be humiliated. Almost invariably these were sited on the green and some remained in use until mid-Victorian times. For the more serious offences the small village lock-up could confine the culprit until his case came before the local court.

Any village that failed to maintain its stocks forfeited the right to hold a market. This and the annual fair of 'Wakes' took place on the green. The 'wakes' for the duration of the local holiday, anything from a day to a fortnight. As well as swings and roundabouts the green would also host bear-baiting, jugglers and performing monkeys.

During the rest of the year the green was a

the village stocks

rendezvous for itinerant travellers, tinkers and gypsies, who would sell their wares on the steps of the market cross. On May Day the maypole was erected upon the green, and Morris dancing and other forms of merriment went on around it.

It was either on the green or in the churchyard that the local lads had to fulfil their weekly commitment of two hours archery practise. Sometimes grooves can be found in the surrounding stone walls where the archers sharpened their arrows.

Part of the village green was taken up by the parish pond. Here the locals would water their animals and youngsters learn how to catch tiddlers. Witches would be immersed in its waters by means of the ducking stool until they confessed, and scolds and gossips until they promised to hold their tongue and amend their ways.

The water was a useful source of supply should any of the thatched roofs catch fire. Drovers also used the pond to refresh their cattle which rested on the green overnight. According to Celtic folklore pixies, elves, goblins, gnomes and fairies danced in the mist on the village green at night when most folk were fast asleep.

It was at the well on the green that the women gathered daily to draw water for drinking and washing, and annually to decorate it with flowers as a 'thank you' gesture to the water spirits for their generosity, a custom which still continues today under the name of 'well-dressing', especially in Derbyshire.

Younger children would get some fresh air into their lungs playing 'tick' or 'leapfrog' on the green, then relax and make daisy chains to garland one another. After school or work older children would play their version of football with discarded caps or jackets to mark the position of the muddy goalmouth. The loan of a farmer's thick hemp cart-rope gave them the opportunity to practice their tug-o-war contest against the neighbouring parish.

Whilst sheep and cattle grazed the outfield the central area of the green was scythed and rolled to provide a pitch for the village cricket team - captained by the squire. Until the 16th Century bowling was underarm and runs were scored by recording notches on a stick. When the parson became a member of the team, the church hymn board and its numbers were used to relay the score to both the supporters and the opposition from the rival village. The squire was also Master of the Foxhounds and once or twice a year they would meet on the green outside the pub for the traditional 'stirrup cup' before 'Tally Ho'ing' off after foxes.

The reduction in both the size and stature of the village green was also proportionate to the increase in its uses. The footpath that once crossed the green gradually became a single width cart track and in recent years was widened to a dual carriageway linking the two local towns. At that time it was considered a better option than installing a bypass around the outskirts and leaving the village isolated. A signpost on the green pointed travellers in the right direction.

For villagers with no transport a 'bus stop' sign was erected and for their further convenience in bad weather, a bus shelter was built. As the thatched houses of the village are photogenic, a lot of sightseers pay a visit. For their convenience toilets and a small tarmaced car park were installed on the green.

In the late Victorian times the village green was the most conveniently situated area on which to build the new school. Its playground was surrounded by spiked iron railings - to keep the children in or the animals out?

Soon after the first World War a large second hand army hut was purchased for use as a village hall. Again it was the communal space on the village green that was the one and only consideration for a site - as it cost nothing.

About this time were added the names of the fallen around the base of the Market Cross which was fenced off and became the War Memorial. It was also on the edge of the green that both the electricity transformer sub-station and the telephone junction box were installed, with their attendant poles, stays and overhead wires that criss-crossed the green.

When the churchyard became full and was is in dire need of extension a further section of the village green disappeared, as did another part when the gypsies who had camped on that same spot for generations decided to take up permanent residence and eventually built a wooden house there.

Still more space went in providing the children with a fenced play area, with its wood chip safety floor. But it lacked the joviality and attraction of the ancient fairground and after a short-lived burst of enthusiasm is now seldom used by the village children.

When 'Dig For Victory' became the wartime slogan part of the green was dug up for allotments to enable the villagers to grow more food. Nearly 60 years on they are still in use. Most of the holders keep their allotments immaculate but the gardening prowess of one or two did lead to a downgrading in the 'Best Kept Village' competition. The plaques denoting successful years are exhibited on a pole beside the green.

Next to it is the 'parish notice board', now sadly needing a lick of paint. It holds notices of past, present and future functions, fluttering in the breeze and held in place by rusty drawing pins, tin tacks or felt nails.

The Post Office-cum shop has had to close owing to lack of trade but the red telephone kiosk remains an integral part of the village green following a spirited petition to preserve it after it was rumoured that it was to be removed and replaced by a modern, trumpet-blowing glass edifice. And still on its original site beside it stands the sturdy red pillar box with the initials 'V.R.' cast into its door.

The squire and the parson no longer live in the parish, their houses have been purchased by richer folk from the towns who can afford to install modern amenities. As a direct result the foxhounds no longer meet on the green opposite the inn and the cricketers have transferred their affections to a new pitch and a level playing field provided by the council at the leisure centre in the local town, which has the distinct advantage of a pavilion with a licensed bar.

Owing to the depleted congregation and the lessening of the influence of the church, the annual 'wakes', formerly celebrated over several days on the green, has now been reduced to an afternoon's 'Garden Party' on the Rector's lawn in the neighbouring town, from where he is now responsible for maintaining the services in three churches owing to recent ecclesiastical amalgamations.

The once busy Smithy became a garage with petrol pumps but that too became uneconomic and with the retirement of the blacksmith has been turned into a private residence. Unfortunately the chestnut tree on the green, whose branches spread to the door of the smithy and under which the elderly sat to discuss the changes in village life, blew down in the hurricane a few years ago. A new bench donated by the W.I. now stands in its place.

The village 'pinfold' in which straying animals were impounded until their owner paid the appropriate fine, the village 'lock-up' and the village 'stocks' all on the green, have been restored to their former glory, though few passers-by realise what they were originally used for.

The village well has been capped over for safety reasons but in its place stands a large, cast iron pump sheltered from the elements by a thatched roof and frequently photographed by visitors. The remaining part of the green has been enclosed by white painted posts linked by lengths of black plastic chain to prevent motorists churning up the grass.

There are a couple of occasions when the green is still used by almost all the community. One is for the bonfire and fireworks on November 5th, or nowadays the nearest convenient weekend. The other is for the erection of the village Christmas tree - adorned with its coloured lights, and weather permitting, the carols are sung around it on the Sunday afternoon before Christmas, though this service is increasingly being held inside the church owing to inclement weather.

Yet, for all its changes, the image that most of us have of the village green is a haven of peace and quiet, a symbol of community spirit, where children can play by day, men can enjoy cricket at night and a refuge where the elderly can sit and watch the rest of the world go by.

Long may it remain.

183 August Rushes
'A VALUABLE RURAL COMMODITY'

'It's all in the genes', or so they say.

In the days before our modern 'throw away' society, communities were self contained, self supporting and almost everything had to be made within the locality. It is amazing how adept people became at utilising common materials to fulfil their everyday needs.

At this time of the year the one that springs immediately to mind is the 'RUSH'. Basically there are two types. The first, JUNCTUS ACUTUS, grows in tight round clumps, two to three feet (a metre) high in boggy, acidic and poorly drained soil. The other, SCIRPUS ACUSTRIC, is found on the banks of ponds, streams and lakes and will grow six to ten feet tall (2-3 metres).

How long their uses have been known can be explained by the biblical story of the baby Moses who floated down the Nile in a cradle of rushes and in the British Museum is a four thousand year old stool from Egypt complete with its seat of woven rushes.

When required for plaiting they were cut with a short bladed scythe from mid-June onwards when the brown plumes first burst into flower. Each batch was cut on alternative years to allow the roots time to recover which resulted in tall, luxuriant growth for the future. Riverside rushes were tied into bundles called bolts of forty two inches (106 cms) and tied in two places with rushes.

The stems were stood upright and leant against wooden racks for about three weeks to dry, then stored in an airy barn. By then they had shrunk by about a third and sometimes

become contaminated with a dry, dusty mould that has a characteristic strong smell which emerges when the rushes are dampened to work them. Stored in the dark they retained their glossy green, sunlight and age bleach them to a pale brown or creamy colour.

Before plaiting the dry stems are soaked in soft water for a minute or two then wrapped in a cloth for a day or so before use. The stems are graded and each one is wiped with a cloth or between the fingers from the tip to butt to remoisten the exterior, flatten the stem and expel surplus air.

There are two main ways of plaiting, a straightforward 'over and under' weave or a 'two plait' twisting them alternatively before and behind the uprights.

Although, having said that, there are many other variations. The earliest example many country folk remember was as a child when given a rush-rattle made from seven or nine field rushes and containing two small stones known as 'dicky birds' which when knocked together produced the clinking noise.

Carpets of rushes were the floor covering of yesteryear. After cleaning out the old smelly, squelchy, flea-ridden material, fresh rushes were strewn on the earthen floors of homes, halls and churches throughout the land. The rich might replace them twice a year but poorer homes, cottages and churches only once, in the summer.

Sweet smelling 'nose' herbs of rosemary, mint, sage and lavender were sometimes added to give it an additional aroma. This annual ceremony largely died out when floorboards came in but is still commemorated by special 'rush-bearing' services held in a few churches and chapels even today. The two which spring easiest to mind are 'Grasmere' in the Lake District and the 'Forest Chapel' at Macclesfield.

An ancient account tells how 'a great pile of rushes was carried to the church in a rush-cart with harvest gearings. It was secured by flower covered ropes, on top was an oak bough and a man who directed the proceedings. In front and beside the cart walked girls who carried flower garlands and rush bearings in the form of crowns, harps and maypoles.

A Morris team in the forefront danced the 'Long Morris' in procession and the 'Cross Morris' at stopping places on the route. The church bells pealed as the sweet smelling reeds were taken down and thickly covered the floor of earth. The rest of the day was a public holiday when the people played games, wrestled and raced, there was gingerbread for the children and 'ribbon fairings' to be won - we now call them 'rosettes'.

In halls and houses people slept on rushes around the central fire. Distinguished guests were given clean rushes, those of inferior standing had to sleep on used rushes or none at all, hence the phrase 'Not worth the rush'. Another very important use for the rush was and still is thatch, but it is highly inflammable, oddments and discarded rushes were widely used to light fires and because of the fire risk, thatch was forbidden in towns from 1212AD.

At night poorer houses were lit by rush light. They were made by removing the majority of the outer rind leaving one or two thin strips lengthwise to hold the centre pith in place. They were dried and when any surplus fat was left over from cooking, the rushes were dipped into the 'scummings' once or twice to give them a tallow coating.

Held in a special easily adjusted holder at an angle of 45-60 degrees, a forty inch (metre) length of rush would burn for up to two hours. Gilbert White, the famous naturalist wrote that 'One and a half pounds of rushes treated in this way would provide a cottage with a meagre light all winter at a fraction of the cost of candles'.

Rush light tapers were used to light the large number of candles used to illuminate churches on winter days. Rushes and fine sand were used to scour armour before battle and to clean pewter after eating. But probably the most pleasing form of rush work comes from plaiting. The only tools required are hand shears, sharp scissors, a packing needle (or Bodkin) with a large eye, a small curved needle for sewing the strips together, some soft brown string, soft soap and a mallet to flatten the plaits.

Rushes are very sensitive to humidity, they work best in warm, moist, muggy weather and plaiting should never be attempted in an East wind, a frost, in front of a fire or in strong sunlight. Thicker reeds are the strongest, they are especially suitable for chair seats and backs, log baskets, housemaids kneelers and after the introduction of floorboards, for plaiting into rush mats where long lengths of plait were curled, coiled, twisted and sewn together into decorative shapes and patterns. As they were so light and portable a roll up rush-mat-mattress would help to accommodate any unexpected visitor overnight. Rushes were also plaited into rope harness and a soft but extremely strong horse collar to break in aggressive colts. Rush beehives almost identical to their straw counterparts were often made in the slack period between the hay and corn harvests.

A rather strange use was by some coopers, who placed a rush between each stave of their barrels. Should the barrel remain empty for a long time it would dry out and shrink. When new wine or beer was put in the long lengths of rush, being hygroscopic, rapidly adsorbed the moisture and expanded to fill the gap, thus immediately making the barrel watertight long before the wood had a chance to swell.

Although plaiting was also done by men it was generally termed 'women's work', girls were taught how to plait from the age of five or six. Women plaiters were called 'Matters' the name given to the strong smell arising from the dampened powdery mould.

They often worked side by side in teams. The long lengths of plait being wound onto a horizontal bar in front of them. On their feet they wore soft, comfortable shoes and sandals made from rushes. Those who lived a distance away carried their food in 'flag baskets', farm workers called them 'frails' - they were made from rushes. I have one which has been used about twice weekly for some twenty years to carry visual aids for one of my talks. It is made from a length of about twelve yards of one and a half inch wide, flat three-plait, stitched into a connected spiral of twelve circles. Apart from fading to pale brown from its original green it has hardly worn at all

All manner of useful objects and containers were made by the industrious hands of the craft people of yesteryear. Platters for food, decorative rush table mats which have recently come back into fashion, plant holders, dressing table tidies with hinged lids, waste paper baskets, rush hats and decorative animals similar to those from abroad sold in Oxfam shops. This emphasises why this craft has largely died out in this country, as a direct result of the poor wages earned by workers and the introduction of modern alternatives.

It is thought that the gentle curves of rush work were responsible for the picturesque intertwining of Celtic artwork on crosses. Rushes were also plaited into rosary beads and intricate, delicate patterns woven into church rush kneelers stuffed with discard ends - called 'HASSOCKS' because this was the Celtic word for the rushes from which they were made.

In church too it always makes me smile when I hear my name referred to in the hymn 'All Things Bright and Beautiful' which mentions - The rushes by the water we gather everyday'.

It is highly probable that my lifetime enthusiasm for plaiting (albeit in straw) evolves from the genes passed on to me by my ancestors who gathered, worked with and lived among the rushes, that is how my surname of RUSH is said to have originated. For as they say 'It's all in the genes'.

184 September Windmills
'A POIGNANT REMINDER OF OUR PAST'

If I were asked what would be amongst the most nostalgic yet inspiring sights anyone could see in the countryside, somewhere very close to the top of my list would have to be a working windmill with the full sweep of its sails whirling around. Even more so if it was set against a backdrop of dark receding storm clouds and centred under the colourful arc of a beautiful double rainbow. That would certainly get the cameras clicking.

Somehow windmills seem to conjure up an image of the freedom of rural life, though for those who built, maintained and worked in them life was often anything but pleasant.

Villagers who lived in the valleys or near flowing streams built watermills to grind their corn, over five and a half thousand are recorded in the Domesday Book, but there are no windmills mentioned.

It is thought that the Arabs invented the idea of harnessing the wind to do the donkey work of raising water to irrigate their arid areas. Whether it was the returning crusaders or merchants who introduced them into England we will never know. Anyhow they arrived and for the next eight hundred years ground grain to provide flour and cattle food for those who lived on the hilltops or on land too flat to provide running water to drive a millwheel.

Each mill served the needs of about fifty families. To gain a bit of extra height they were often built on the raised moulds of barrows or tumuli. The earliest windmills were made entirely of wood, they were rectangle in shape and had a ridged roof, oak beams, elm flooring, cladding and bins.

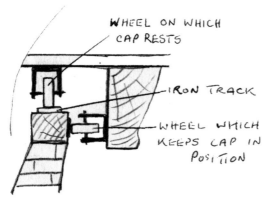

WHEEL ON WHICH CAP RESTS

IRON TRACK

WHEEL WHICH KEEPS CAP IN POSITION

The whole heavy clumsy structure rotated on a pivot of a strongly braced central oak 'tree-trunk' sized post. As a result they were called 'post-mills'. The whole of this heavy top portion had to be manually turned to set the sails into the 'eye of the wind' by a long 'tailpole' which projected from the rear.

Windmill 'sails' are so called because the wooden framework was originally covered with canvas sailcloth to make it resist the wind sufficiently to turn the gearing and the grinding stones.

The sails were attached to a 18 degree sloping 'windshaft'. The angle helped to throw some of the weight of the sails to the centre of the mill and also miss the wider foundations.

Along the windshaft was a large diameter, dual purpose, wooden toothed gear wheel which intermeshed with a cog wheel which turned the upright shaft that ran vertically through the mill. Another large gear wheel attached to this shaft turned smaller gear wheels called 'stone nuts' which rotated the top 'runner stone'. The bottom stone, fastened to the floor, was known as the 'bed stone'.

The outside of the dual purpose gear wheel acted as an essential brake drum when shaped wooden blocks were pressed onto it if a sudden gust of wind started to turn the sails too fast.

Care had to be taken not to apply the brake too long or too often for the friction of the wood caused considerable heat and might start a fire and certainly on hilltops there was no readily available source of water to douse the flames.

There were many other drawbacks to being a miller in those days. In winter cold winds blew draughts through every crack in the weatherboarded exterior, he had to keep working to keep himself warm. The sails needed constant attention.

The strength of the wind determined how much area of sail was covered with canvas. A strong wind, a quarter, a medium wind, a half light wind, a three quarters to full. These positions were called first reef, sword point, dagger point and full. Each sail had to be similarly covered or it would be out of balance.

If the wind either rose or lessened during milling the canvas area had to be altered accordingly. To do this the miller had to apply the brake to stop the sails turning. He then had to climb the sail nearest to the ground, reset the canvas and lash it securely with its ropes, climb down, release the brake to allow the next sail to become vertical, apply the brake, climb the sail, set the canvas and so on, remember there were 'four' sails, some mills had either six or even eight for extra power.

Energetic young millers sometimes climbed both vertical sails at one stop but this was dangerous in gusty winds when the top stood anything from sixty to eighty feet above ground. Those afraid of heights only climbed one sail at a time.

The task was doubly dangerous in driving rain or frosty weather when the wooden bars were treacherously slippery, the canvas and ropes frozen solid and feet and fingers numb with cold. But it had to be done when there was a wind.

There were far too many days in the year when the mill stood idle for lack of wind and the villagers were crying out for flour to bake their bread. After a calm spell, when the wind did finally arrive the miller often worked through the night to catch up with the demand, though all too frequently the strength of the wind faded away as the sun went down.

Another drawback was that he had to keep moving the mill around to face the sails square on to the wind, a heavy task often needing block and tackle (ropes and pulleys). As mills grew larger a horse or donkey was often kept permanently harnessed to pull the mill round. The ladder by which the mill was entered also had to be lifted clear of the ground every time the mill was turned.

Most demanding of all was that he had to carry every sack of grain on his back up the ladder and right to the top of the mill where it was tipped into the hoppers that slowly emptied along vibrating 'clacking damsel' chutes that fed a slow but steady stream of grain into the centre of the millstones.

The scissor action of the stones reduced the grain to a smooth flour which emerged into troughs around the circumference. It dropped down a chute onto a vibrating sieve which sorted the coarser bran, the outer husk, from the finer white flour, that was stored in the flour 'boulter' until being bagged up for collection by the customer.

In order to make the mill more stable the whole of the intricate base timbers were embedded in soil, but this made it rot faster. Later the base was supported on 4, 6 or 8 stone or brick piers, just above the ground and protected from the weather by a circular brick or stone building, a roundhouse, which was used for additional storage. The mill wore an extended skirt or petticoat of weather-boarding to keep its sides waterproof and cover the gap between the mill and the roundhouse. A couple of potential disasters were fire caused when the stones ran 'dry' - out of grain, and because windmills were high and exposed they were liable to be struck by lightning or blown over in a severe storm, especially if the tailpole was not fastened securely, when the sails might swivel away from the wind and either be blown off or badly damaged.

In order for the wind to turn the sails they had to be set at a slightly twisted angle, rather like a modern aeroplane propeller. The best 'weathering' angle was found to be 22 degrees at the centre tapering to 7 degrees at the tip. In a steady wind the sails would turn between eight and twelve times a minute, which turned the millstones between forty and sixty times a minute. Most sails swept round in an anti-clockwise direction to make it easier for the miller or millwright to groove the millstones clockwise with his 'mill bill and thrift'.

Some of the early sails had a projection board on the leading edge for streamlining, the sailcloth being fastened to the trailing edge. To increase power by almost a quarter other sails had a triangular extension added to the leading edge making the sails five feet wide at the tip. Everyone had to be wary of the windmills massive sail arms, since their thirty foot length circled only a few feet from the ground and would knock anything over that stood in its way.

When the mills were built higher this problem no longer existed but in order to reach the bottom of the sails a balcony, supported by struts, was built around the tower to enable the miller to reach and climb them.

As the years passed new inventions eased some of the cumbersome workload of the miller. From the windshaft a friction operated hoist now lifted his heavy sacks of grain to the top storage hoppers. Someone else had the idea of just revolving the sails and windshaft in a separate 'cap' on wheels on top of the structure, instead of the whole mill. This made the task of setting the sails into the wind much easier as it could now be done with a circular rack and pinion operated by a endless chain.

As the top had now to be circular the whole mill changed shape, from rectangular to octagonal or even twelve sided. The outside was clad in white painted timber weatherboards and from a distance the tapering sides surmounted by a black tarred canvas covered wooden 'cap' looked like a countryman in his traditional costume, so thereafter they were known as 'smock' mills. In order to turn the 'cap' automatically a small 'fantail' of six or eight sails was erected at right angles to the sails (and the direction of the wind) at the rear of, and geared to the cap.

Instead of wood some mills were built more solidly of brick or stone, these were conical and called 'tower mills' and are the most common kind now found around the countryside.

At the same time developments were also happening to improve the 'common' canvas covered sails. In 1722 a Scotsman - Miekle - who also invented a threshing machine, introduced a new type of spring operated sail. It had a series of hinged canvas or wooden shutters all connected to a long iron bar attached to the spring.

It acted like a venetian blind, opening to let the wind spill through during a gust, then closing by action of the spring when the wind subsided, so regulating the speed of the sails. But the tension still had to be adjusted from the tip of the sail blades, which meant applying the brake, stopping the mill and adjusting each sail in turn.

About fifty years later an engineer, William Cubitt, designed a 'Patent' crank system connection with all four sail mechanisms at the centre and passing along a rod down a hole bored along the windshaft and controlled from inside the mill by weights or a centrifugal governor. This web of connecting mechanisms was called a 'spider' and meant that at last the sails could be controlled whilst the millstones were working.

The advent of steam power, the purchase of large quantities of grain from abroad and the building of new and powerful iron grinding rollers at the ports put paid to the life of the picturesque windmill. The majority slowly decayed and disintegrated. A few have been partially reclaimed, most of which have a non-rotating open sail frame. They are so costly to maintain that hardly any have sails in working order.

Perhaps it is because there are so few to be seen that they arouse such nostalgic memories of a past age - the age of the windmill.

185 October Mushrooms
'PART OF NATURE'S BOUNTY'

When you were young did you love to look at pictures of fairies dancing on the grass with an audience of elves sitting on a surrounding ring of toadstools?

Or perhaps you marvelled at the marauding Viking warriors who believed they were infallible and wore no protective armour, only their bearskin coat?

Why were the 'hippies' wandering around the countryside, what were they searching for? And what was behind the belief that Santa Claus and his reindeer flew through the air to deliver the Christmas presents to children? Well in every case the answer boils down to one basic ingredient - mushrooms.

Quite a few years ago I remember a group of true Romany gypsies going ecstatic when they found a great clump of brown fungi growing from the side of the stump of a dead tree on my farm. When I enquired why it was that they almost worshipped them, yet I could hardly care less for them, they told me it was because they originated from the continent with all its woods and trees and so were brought up in the ways of the forest and the food it provided free of charge.

In this country our ancestors cut down the trees to make open fields. That is why today, unless we have been educated otherwise, we only eat field mushrooms that grow in the open and in the light, and have an inherited prejudice against the three thousand or more other varieties that have any connection with the dark, haunting forests.

The ones WE eat we call mushrooms, those we don't we term toadstools, perhaps because this name infers something unpalatable, even though only about twenty kinds are poisonous and only a handful of those are FATAL.

Mushrooms were considered 'meat' for the poor man, their only cost being the time spent gathering them. They were regarded more as a delicacy rather than a meal. The appetite for mushrooms on the continent was so great it was once considered a 'French disease', which was emphasised in 1754 when an epidemic of poisoning around Paris led to a law forbidding their gathering and sale. But such was the demand that the peasants defied the ruling and kept picking them.

The fact that some tasty varieties may be regarded as poisonous in one country yet highly acclaimed in another may be accounted for by the different digestive juices that each country has according to its diet. For even the most deadly ones of all can be eaten by slugs, snails, rabbits and rodents without any ill-effect - or so I've been told.

Many of the poisonous toxins they contain are eliminated during drying and cooking, but they should not be eaten by people suffering from arthritis, gout or in conjunction with alcohol or rich animal proteins. In other words, preferably with fish, fruit, salads and vegetables. A hundred years ago 'rickets' deformed the bones of many town dwellers while those in the country who ate mushrooms, often obtained sufficient vitamin D to help counteract this disease.

Our lovely green countryside is kept alive by photosynthesis, plants use sunlight to convert carbon dioxide and water into complicated foods in the form of 'sap'. Fungi act in reverse, they break down complex substances into simple ones. They digest decaying matter into a compost so that bacteria can move in and continue the process.

A simple example of this in action is that about a ton of leaf litter falls for every acre of woodland annually. If it wasn't for the fungi and bacteria the trees would eventually disappear under a carpet of their own waste. Left entirely to nature it takes about twenty years for a fallen tree to completely decompose.

Fungi can also live as a parasite on a tree and obtain all its nutrients as in the case of the oak tree by my gate on which grows a bracket fungus whose colour and

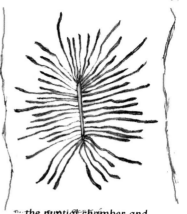

the nuptial chamber and feeding galleries of the Dutch elm beetle grub - the beetle that carries the fungus which killed our elm trees

texture makes it look exactly what it is called, a 'beefsteak' fungus, it even drips a red liquid when cut. The staining that this fungus imparts to the interior of the tree makes the wood highly sought after by cabinet makers. When old and leathery, the skin of one fungus was used to put an extra keen edge on razors, hence its name, the 'razor strop fungus'. Another bracket-type fungus is called 'Jew's ear' and grows on elderberry trees. Its original name was 'Judas ear' because Judas was supposed to have hanged himself from a elderberry after betraying Jesus, a story which is completely untrue because elderberries do not grow in the Holy Land.

The majority of fungi obtain their food from a living host, a union which is beneficial to both. It works like this. Thousands upon thousands of extremely tiny fungal threads called 'hyphae' grow through the soil. They colonise and cover the fine roots of trees with a cobweb-like net.

These threads are so minute that they penetrate between the individual cells of the roots. They extract nourishment from the tree in the form of sap sugars which enable it to spread and flourish. In return the fungal threads absorb water and essential minerals from a far greater area of the surrounding soil than the tree roots could possibly accomplish on their own and feed these ingredients into the sap system of the tree. Each relies on the other for its existence and it is especially beneficial to trees which grow on poorer soil such as beech, birch, lime and pines.

The hyphae's threads work away unseen underground all year long until some become so swollen with autumn rains falling on the warm soil that they throw up their fruiting bodies in the form of mushrooms, toadstools or fungi in such a colourful array of shapes and sizes. That is why certain types are always found near their companion tree hosts.

Apart from spreading by their multitude of underground hyphae threads, fungi also disperse their spores in a variety of ways. Mushrooms and toadstools grow on slender stalks which lift spore-bearing gills on the underside of their umbrella-shaped dome, just above the layer of calm air at ground level into the more turbulent currents that will carry the microscopic pores away to colonise new food sources.

When I was at infant school I once took a very large, dark and ripe horse-mushroom to show my teacher. She laid it on a sheet of white paper. Next morning she said if all the children in the class tapped on it, something magical would happen. With eager anticipation we did and when she lifted it up, there on the paper was the exact imprint of its radiating gills - in spores - until one of the lads sneezed and blew a cloud of black 'dust' everywhere.

Puff-balls are soft, spongy and edible when young. As they age the outer skin becomes thin and leathery, the inside is filled with spores. When raindrops impact on the outer skin it acts like a miniature bellows and expels a 'puff' of spores through a pore in the top of its head. Old time beekeepers used the smoke from smouldering puff ball spores to quieten their bees when examining hives or extracting honey.

The 'stinkhorn' uses another method of spore dispersal. It grows a jelly-like ball similar to a snake's egg which, when ripe, suddenly grows a single stem to a height of about six inches (15cms) within a couple of hours. Its knobbed end is covered with spores in a stinking slime which is very attractive to flies who converge onto it, eat the slime and discrete it some distance away. Because this fungus looks exactly like a phallic symbol it was widely prized and made into love philtres and aphrodisiacs. It was also fed to cattle to improve their fertility, though I must say I never tried it on my cows.

A fungi that has tight curls at the bottom of its cap as it emerges was known as the 'lawyer's wig'. After a day or so the curls degenerate and drop a dark fluid which was once used for writing, hence its more unusual name 'shaggy ink cap', whilst one with spines is nicknamed 'hedgehog fungus'.

A very useful find in bygone days was the 'tinder box' fungus which when dry would readily ignite a spark. On dead ash branches in my furthers fields I would often find charcoal black balls which when dried burned fiercely. They were known as 'King Alfred's cakes' for obvious reasons, also 'cramp balls' because they were once carried in countrymen's pockets to alleviate that complaint.

'Bootlace' or 'boney' fungus can be collected in handfuls on and under dead and dying bark on trees. It glows in the dark and was sometimes used as way markers on woodland paths at night.

Two fungi that are highly beneficial are penicillin and yeast, while a tasty one is truffles, found underground and believed by our ancestors to be formed where lightning had struck the ground.

'shaggy inkcap'

But to return to my opening paragraph, 'fairy rings' started as a single fungus whose hyphae threads radiated outwards from the central point at about six inches (15 cms) a year.

I had several on one field that were about 12ft (4 metres), the largest recorded is 164ft or 50 metres diameter and about 300 years old. The nutrients are all used up in the central area and grasses there become stunted or die. The excessive activity of hyphae threads on the outer edge produce extra fertility hence lush grass and after rain a ring of toadstools which elves and fairies were supposed to use as stools or parasols.

The red capped mushroom with white flecks on which fairies are usually pictured is the 'fly agaric', so named because it was once crushed with milk and used as a fly killer. It is this mushroom that the hippies searched for. Taken in small quantities it gives hallucinations, especially of strength, bravery and of floating on air.

It was this dried fungi that caused the Viking warriors to go 'berserk', a word which simply meant the bearskin coat which they wore when under the influence and on the attack, although afterwards the 'high' feeling changed into an extremely 'low' depression. This could be counteracted by taking another dose to give another high and so on and so on.

Laplanders discovered that their reindeer sought out and ate 'fly agaric' and became 'high'. They collected the reindeers' urine, distilled it, drank the alcoholic product and became 'high' themselves. Thus the belief began that if both Santa and his reindeer ate the magic mushrooms they could fly around the world to deliver their presents on time at Christmas.

HIC

By a strange coincidence when I was researching this subject last year I met a man from Scandinavia who told me that 'fly agaric' was gathered in the autumn, dried and pickled in spirits. A small tipple of it was taken every day during Advent and the remainder drunk late on Christmas Eve, which meant that everyone was on a 'high' for the midwinter solstice. I am therefore writing this article early so that you will have time to prepare for your Christmas celebrations!

186 November Tractors
'A FARMERS BEST FRIEND'

The tractor has probably contributed more to progress on the farm than any other invention.

Man first cultivated the ground with the aid of animals, especially pigs, to turn the earth over. He levelled the soil, sowed his seeds and hoped for the best. Afterwards, to cultivate small areas the farmer would push a breast plough which would disturb the top few inches.

His wife and family helped by pulling the implement from the front. It must have been quite a relief to them when oxen were trained to pull the pointed stump through the earth instead.

Almost all kinds of animals have at some time been adapted to this task, including elephants, camels and donkeys.

At first oxen then eventually horses became the main means of motivation. Their pulling power made them ideal for draught work. Their main drawback was that a considerable proportion of the farm acreage had to be devoted to growing grass, hay, roots and oats especially to feed them.

Then last century large numbers of skilled countrymen left the land to work in industry, increasing the burden of work on those left behind.

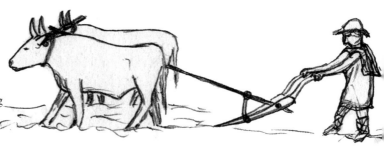

In order that the essential routines of each farming season could be undertaken and completed with fewer workers meant that the existing manpower had to be used more effectively which is where mechanisation gradually came in.

The earliest attempts at ploughing using steam traction engines were very costly and not very successful. The weight of the engine meant it could not travel on the field so stood stationary on the headland with a squared system of cables and pulleys rigged to pull the plough.

But the pulleys pulled out of place, the cables snapped or slipped off the winding drum and chaos ensued.

Some of these problems were overcome when TWO engines worked from opposite headlands pulling the multi-fullowed reversible plough back and forth between them. Although it did need large, level fields it was a method operated for a great many years. It was found that steam traction was more suited to heavy haulage of wagons on the road than cultivating farm fields.

About a hundred years ago an engine was invented that did not need to convert water to steam, it ran on ordinary household lamp oil. The oil intake had to be heated with a blowlamp to start it, but once hot it would run indefinitely. The 'stationary engine' had arrived.

It was used for driving all kinds of farm-barn machinery threshers, millers, grinders, rollers, root pulpers, hay and straw cutters, but it was not portable.

The first self-propelled paraffin engine was a 24 horse-power 'Ivel' three wheeler, which demonstrated its prowess in 1902 by pulling two binders and cutting seventeen acres of corn in six hours, a notable achievement even by today's standards. A great advance came when it was discovered that engines could be started easier and without preheating on petrol and when warmed up changed over to the much cheaper paraffin.

The tractor industry expanded rapidly both here and in America. But except for a few progressive farmers most were wary and slow to change. They preferred to keep their change in their pockets for most of the tractors on offer cost upwards of three hundred pounds and about half of them were too heavy for field work except in ideal conditions.

One kind which did not make such a mess and sink into the soil, laid its own tracks and then ran on them in a continuous belt. It would even pull its plough through heavy clay in sticky conditions and override most obstacles. During the First World War Winston Churchill suggested they should be armour-plated, carry troops and fire guns. To the troops they became known as 'tanks' and to post-war farmers 'caterpillar' tractors.

By the 1920s most of the items taken for granted on modern tractors were already in production on some make or other. Ball bearings, multi-speed gearboxes, self starter motors, independent brakes, pedal operated clutches, electric lighting for night work and power take off with pulley attachment to drive barn machinery or attached implements.

By now Henry Ford was supplying about half the tractors in circulation. But the agricultural depression had also arrived, farmers were even more reluctant to part with their hard earned money.

An outstanding tractor problem was the ability of the smooth steel wheels to grip the ground. 'V' shaped metal 'spuds' or angled 'cleats' were bolted into the rims, or 'strakes' were fastened onto the hubs, but if they travelled on tracks or roads they cut them up and did a tremendous amount of damage.

Consequently a steel slip ring had to be bolted over them if they went onto the highway, all of which was time consuming. In the early 1930s 'Firestone' developed a cleated pneumatic tyre and very soon most tractors were 'running on air' so to speak. Lighter tractor weights also meant that most cultivations could now be carried out without causing soil compaction.

However on most farms horses were still being used to 'set out' the field, plough the first furrows and finish off. The tractor ploughed the land in between the furrows.

The big breakthrough in tractor design came when the inventive son of an Irish farmer, who was interested in cars and mechanics and had built and flown the first aeroplane in Ireland was appointed to maintain Irish tractors in World War One.

He found most of them heavy, cumbersome and difficult to use especially in conjunction with antiquated horse implements. He had the idea of combining the implement with the tractor and in 1920 with this in mind he designed a three point linkage system which would transfer part of the weight and the draught of the attached implement onto the rear driving wheels of the tractor, greatly increasing their grip and improving their efficiency.

It took him a further fifteen years to develop and patent the idea and integrate it with a foolproof hydraulic lifting system. His prototypes were built in Belfast and the main model at Huddersfield, production stopped there during the 1939-45 war but was continued by 'Fords' in America. Exactly fifty years ago in 1946, he set up a factory in Coventry and started mass-producing the most famous little tractor ever made. His name was Harry FERGUSON.

Servicemen returning from the war didn't wish to return to the footslogging routine of following heavy horses, the lightweight little 25hp grey 'Fergy' captured their admiration and soon became the most usual all purpose tractor to be found on Market Gardens, small-holdings and small farms.

Farmers sons were cajoled into staying at home on the farm when father bought them a 'Fergy'. In fact a cousin of mine used his so much and was on it so often that the family nicknamed him 'Fergy' a name which he still acknowledges today.

My future father in law bought a second hand 'Fergy' soon after I joined his workforce. I inherited it on his death and it is the only tractor I have ever had. In a few years it will have been in service for half a century and it is still in good working order having done every job asked of it whatever the weather and however bad the conditions.

Harry Ferguson's earliest models ran very efficiently on petrol, later models like mine were fitted with a duel fuel tank, petrol was used for starting and when the engine was hot the tap was turned over to the T.V.O. tank - Tractor Vaporising Oil - a special grade of paraffin.

In recent times the tendency has been for tractors to run on the even less expensive diesel fuel. They have become bigger, heavier and far more complicated with lots of additional gadgets designed for the 'comfort' of the isolated driver. Most are fitted with cabs, heaters, radios and mobile phones as standard.

Yet with all their 'mod cons' they are not held in the same esteem as the open, sturdy, reliable mechanical workhorse of post war Britain, which in spite over three million being produced I have never yet heard anyone speak badly of them. Those faithful, trustworthy, little grey 'Fergy' tractors.

And just to prove that they have 'come of age', they are now regularly found at vintage rallies, a nostalgic reminder, if one were needed, that those of us who worked with them and held them in such affection are rapidly reaching those same vintage years ourselves.

187 December Pigs
'THE USEFUL PIG - MAN'S GOOD FRIEND FOR 6000 YEARS'

Although I don't suppose that a boar's head will feature as the centrepiece of your Christmas table, it did occupy that position of prominence for hundreds of years.

It all came about because people believed that 'Freyr', the Celtic God of 'Peace and Plenty', rode through the heavens on a wild boar called Gullibursti.

Consequently, at Yuletide, or as we now call it, Christmas, a wild boar was ceremoniously hunted, sacrificed and eaten in his honour.

The history of the pig is far more intricate and interesting than many might at first imagine. As I have mentioned several times before - 'Pigs were the bulldozers of antiquity and sheep the mowing machines that followed behind.'

Six thousand years ago herds of pigs trampled down the reeds and trod in the corn and cotton seeds in Egypt. Pigs were sacred to the Greeks, who sacrificed one to Demeter at the beginning of the corn harvest and another to Bacchus, the God of wine, before the vintage.

The Romans relished pork. They fattened their pigs on figs to improve their flavour and honey to bloat their livers. In the wild the boar was considered as dangerous as the wolf and because of its ferocious fighting ability, the wild boar became the emblem of the 20th Legion.

Socially pigs get on very well together which is why they can be herded. In olden times forests were so widespread and wild pigs so plentiful there was little incentive to domesticate them. Those that were tamed often roamed the forest from midsummer to midwinter. They were also turned out to mate with wild boars after farrowing.

Pigs were the axis of Saxon agriculture. At the time of the Norman Conquest, 1066, pigs were so reliant on the products of the forest floor that Doomsday records the value of woodland according to the number of pigs it would support. At that time there were more pigs in England than people.

The wealthy liked pig meat because it was available fresh all the year. As the number of pigs increased the area of forests decreased, the wild boar was hunted into extinction and pigs became more and more domesticated.

At first their sties were built in the forest clearings but, in the course of time, they moved adjacent to the manor houses and monasteries, nearer their new food supplies. Some piglets were fed with whey and corn gruel, killed at four weeks old, roasted whole and eaten as 'suckling' pigs.

Townspeople also kept pigs and they were allowed to roam the streets from midday to sunset on Saturday while their sties were cleaned out.

Pigs owned by monks and religious houses were called 'St Anthony's swine' because of a tradition going back seventeen hundred years to the founder of Monasticism. Whilst Anthony was a hermit in the Egyptian desert he overcame the temptations of the Devil by making friends with a pig instead of eating it. As a result he became the Patron Saint of pigs. Monasteries which bore his name were allowed to run their pigs loose in the streets to gobble up the garbage thrown out by the householders. They also had special grazing rights. As proof of ownership all 'St Anthony's Swine' wore a bell identifying them and also to scare away evil influences. When they had grown fat they were killed to feed the poor.

In the 1100s an irritating hot weather disease called erysipelas spread across Europe. The painful complaint, which I can testify to from personal experience as I once caught it from one of my pigs, is also called 'diamonds' - and 'St. Anthony's Fire'.

The symptoms are dark diamond-shaped, burning rashes that can prove fatal to cattle, pigs and humans. However, I seem to have survived. The treatment was to pray to St Anthony and rub the affected areas with hard lard to take the 'fire' away.

The spa-springs of Bath were discovered because pigs were wallowing in the waters to cool their eruptions. The smallest pig in the litter the 'Runt' was dedicated to St Anthony in the hope that he might help it to survive. And incidentally, the five black marks surrounding the hairy holes on a pig's front legs are attributed to the story of the Gaderean swine in the Bible (St. Mark v.11-15) - they are the Devil's claw marks.

Although it was generally believed the filthier the pig the tastier the pork, left to themselves pigs are amazingly clean animals. The Gloucester Old Spot was also known as the Orchard Pig because in that county it fattened on windfall apples and, to my mind, there's nothing tastier then a bit of apple with your pork.

Up to the 18th century, our indigenous pigs were largely ungainly, slab-sided, rangy creatures taking up to two years to mature to bacon weight. The nearest similar looking pig today is the ginger Tamworth which was a cross with a Red Indian breed. It has a snout which is so long it was said to be able to 'pick a-pea out of a pint pot'.

Imports of small, prick-eared, fast-maturing black and white Chinese and Italian pigs changed the conformation completely when crossed with our native breeds.

The blacks became the Saddlebacks of Essex and Wessex which I used to keep outside all year round. They were of such a hardy nature, regular breeders and excellent mothers, that they produced an average of three litters of ten piglets every two years for up to 20 years on free

range - but would only last about four years under modern intensive management systems.

Another cross became the Berkshire black, which had a white snout and trotters. The boar was the role model for the tyrant Napoleon in George Orwell's Animal Farm and the female Pigling Bland in the books by Beatrix Potter. Chinese Whites, when crossed through a boar called Sampson, founded the most popular pig in England, the Large White. They are three times more efficient at converting food into meat than any other animal.

Their hams graced the tables of the rich and their fat bacon filled the bellies of the poor to such an extent that the countryman was called a 'Chewbacon' by his city cousins.

Countrymen often spent half an hour a day fondling their pig, many gave them a weekly bath on a Saturday night. Because the cost of feeding a pig ate into the cottager's income it was said there was not much profit in keeping a pig but at least it provided six months good company. Others called it 'the Gentleman that paid the rent'. In late November and December large numbers of pigs were walked along the droving trails to the major seaports, at a pace of about ten miles per day. There they were killed, salted down and put into barrels to provide sustenance for sailors at sea.

Although pigs can be very obstinate - 'pig headed' - they do have many good attributes. They are immensely strong, highly intelligent and possess a powerful sense of smell. In France they are trained to sniff out truffles growing two or three feet underground. In Scotland they were regularly harnessed to pull the plough which they did with more energy than most other animals.

Eccentric landlords used them to warm their bed before retiring, that was if the maid wasn't willing. Some pigs shared their bed and shared their meals. They even went to church together. One particular farmer created a stir when he drove a chaise-cart pulled by a team of four hogs at a brisk trot into St Albans on market day. Crowds turned out to see the unusual sight. The farmer said it had only taken him six months to train them to the shafts - less time than horses.

Pig racing was once very popular. A certain Dutch pig 'Nero' was bet against a trotting horse over a long course from the Hague to the sea. To get the pig into shape the owner walked him along the avenue on the first day and, on arriving at the finishing post, rewarded him with a dish of herrings, his favourite meal. Next day the pig covered the course on its own and again receved its reward. As the days passed the pig got slimmer and his speed got faster, until on the appointed day of the race, to the excitement and astonishment of the large crowd, the pig won, by half a mile.

Probably the most famous pig of all happened quite by accident. A couple of gamekeeper brothers named Toomer were trying to train a batch of dogs to the gun in the New Forest but were getting very little response, when up wandered the gamekeeper's pet pig 'Slut' that he had been given when it was three months old.

One of the bystanders jokingly remarked that it might be easier to train the pig, she certainly couldn't be any worse. The gamekeeper considered it a challenge and, with the help of tit-bits, Slut was responding to her name by the next day and within two weeks she was as good as his best dog.

With her sensitive nose, Slut could point partridges, rabbits and snipe at a distance of forty yards. Soon she regularly hunted and retrieved with the guns on moorland, forest and heath. She slept in the forest at night and galloped out when the keeper called or whistled her and was delighted whenever she saw the gun.

When she was five years old her master died and she was sold with his dogs to a sporting baronet. She was sold again at ten years old. By now the name of Slut was a legend and crowds came to see her in action. Although she was becoming over-fat and rather slothful she could still 'point' as well as ever. Her demise came after she was accused of raiding flocks and killing lambs.

There are a whole host of accounts of children riding their pet pigs - my wife used to push hers around in a pram. One of the highlights of the annual wakes was the tremendous fun that ensued when a greased pig was set free among the crowd. The person who could catch it and hold it aloft for all to see could claim it as his prize. Until a few years ago bowling for a pig was the main attraction for the men at the skittle alley at our village fete. The prize was a weaned piglet presented by a local farmer.

The heaviest pig ever recorded, a hog - a castrated boar - tipped the scales at twelve hundredweight (over 600kgs). It stood over four feet high and was ten feet long.

Even if your festive fare does not include a hog's head, may I wish you 'Peace and Plenty' and every happiness this coming Christmastide.

1997

188 January Frost Fairs
'TALES FROM FROSTY TIMES'

'Ice in November to bear a duck, the rest of the winter slutch and muck' goes the old saying. In some winters this has been true but certainly not the present one.

After an absence of many years the Ice King and the Snow Queen have returned with a vengeance and have kept us in their frosty grip for several weeks.

Nowadays we are inclined to believe we are insulated from most extremes of climatic conditions by modern technology. After all we have thermal clothing, central heating, efficient food distribution and transport systems. But every advantage seems to carry a corresponding disadvantage, apart from having to pay for the privilege.

For instance, take running water. When I was young we NEVER suffered from a burst pipe in the house, soaking carpets and causing chaos. Why? Because all our water was drawn from a well by the back door, we didn't have any water pipes in the farmhouse where I was born!

If the electricity supply fails today, life rapidly grinds to a halt in the majority of households. There is no lighting, no heating, no means of cooking and worst of all for some reason, no television for entertainment.

We never had to bother about these things even during the severest storms or blizzards in the past, for a combination fireplace - 'cooking range' - and oven provided our heat and meals, an oil lamp illuminated indoors and hurricane lanterns outside.

On cold winter's nights we played card games, 'Happy Families' and 'Snap', made Meccano models, grew excited over winning 'Ludo' or 'Snakes and Ladders' and assembled jigsaws.

Our parents either joined in or relaxed, read the papers or books (which in those days usually had a happy ending), mum and granny often sewed dresses, mended socks, embroidered pictures or made rugs. There was a constant flow of conversation, an art that is sadly lacking in many homes today.

We didn't bother about not having an electric blanket to take the chill off our bed, we heated a large stone or brick on the hob, or put a hot water bottle in its knitted cover to stop it scorching our feet and took a candle to guide us up the steep, dark stairs.

Even a moderate fall of snow blocks the roads with skidding cars and causes mayhem to commuters. Far heavier falls were dismissed as of little consequence in the past because most people lived within easy walking distance of work.

Once ploughing had been completed, the main outside activities on the farm in winter were hedging, ditching and manure carting. In very bad weather the men flailed sheaves of corn in the barn, but a continuation of wintry or wet weather might cause them to be laid off and created extra hardships.

The introduction of mechanical equipment especially that which was designed to thresh corn faster and more efficiently was seen by many as a threat to their jobs, which is why they formed gangs and went around rioting and smashing machines in the early to middle 1800s.

At home, an ever constant problem was the need to find sufficient fuel to keep the fire ablaze. As another saying reminds us 'When frost will not suffer to dyke and hedge, then get thee a heat with thy beetle and wedge'. Also, 'Let workman at night bring home wood or log, let none come home empty save slut and dog'.

Splitting firewood with a large and heavy wooden mallet - a beetle - by knocking in iron wedges to reduce the thick tree trunks into usable logs was warming work, equally as warming when cutting and carrying them home as when sitting by the fire and enjoying the blaze. Because of the difficulty of rekindling a fire it was seldom allowed to go out. At night it was banked up with slower burning wet wood, wet leaves or as we sometimes used to do, covered with thick sods of damp turf.

Then, as now, when farmers feared that heavy snow might fall, outlying cattle and sheep were brought on to the farmstead or fields within easy reach. But again, then as now, there were times when it arrived without warning. In those circumstances it was a case of going out and searching for the sheep. Some would be huddled in the lee of hedges or walls, others buried beneath deep drifts.

This is where the long shaft of the shepherd's crook came in handy, to poke through the snow to find the holes in which the sheep were entombed, and, if at night, to hang his lantern from the end whorl of the iron crook to give him a bit of light while he dug them out.

About fifteen years ago dozens of cars and lorries became stuck in drifts whilst trying to beat a blizzard on our main road - the blizzard won. That was the year when our little stream froze from bank to bank allowing my cattle to walk across without cracking the ice. About a hundred years previously the landlord of 'The Golden Cross' formerly an inn and where I now live, accepted the challenge to ride across the frozen lake at Redesmere on horseback. The ice was so thick that he won his wager.

An agricultural book first published about the time called the 'Records of the seasons, Prices of agricultural produce and Phenomena observed in the British Isles' - gives some graphic details of how the weather, both drought and drenching, blazing heat and extreme cold - affected the crops, the cattle and the health of men and animals.

The earliest record in 220AD, states that a tremendous frost in England lasted for five months - and we complain about five weeks! In 353AD a great flood occurred in Cheshire, over five thousand people and a great many cattle perished. There are frequent accounts of intense frosts lasting two months or more, accompanied by heavy snows, which if they thawed rapidly or at the same time as a deluge, resulted in severe flooding and loss of life.

Snowdrifts accumulating from up to eighteen days of blizzards sometimes reached depths of forty to fifty feet.

Occasionally wintry conditions lasted into summer. In 1749 two inches of snow fell at Stockport on June 16th and ice formed thick enough to bear a dog, yet in spite of that the harvest was reported as excellent.

Slightly more recently several spells of snow fell in Cheshire during June 1938. January of that year saw twenty-one days of continuous gales. On three occasions they reached hurricane force with winds of over 100 mph, leaving ten foot snowdrifts in their wake and in October another gust was recorded at 180mph.

Apart from famine one feature which repeatedly comes to the fore is the number of times our larger rivers were frozen over, some forty mentions, many included seaports stating that ships were unable to leave as they were frozen up.

On nine occasions the Thames was frozen so solid that people set up 'Frost Fairs' on the ice. In 1564 Queen Elizabeth led her courtiers around its pleasures which included ox-roasting, fairground attractions, juggling acts, puppet plays and many tradesmen of the city who had erected booths and shops on the ice.

A game of football was played, all in addition to the usual sledging and skating - skates which were of bone; metal skates were introduced from Holland a hundred years later.

Another Frost Fair was held between Christmas and mid February 1740, the ice being nine feet thick and the frost so severe that trees were split asunder as if struck by lightning. Deeply sunken wells were covered with impenetrable ice, crows and other birds fell to the ground frozen in their flight. Bread was as cold and hard as a stone. Beer and ale were frozen within houses and cellars, they were sold by weight and melted in front of the fire. Many hens, ducks and even cattle in the stalls died of cold.

In 1684 a great frost which had begun in December continued for a further eight weeks. The river Thames was frozen over by 9th January and streets of shops stretched from bank to bank. Horses, carts and coaches crossed over on the ice. Charles II attended with his wife and family, sheep and oxen were roasted whole, bull baiting, horse and coach races and a full blown foxhunt were held.

A printing press was set up and for sixpence people could purchase a souvenir sheet of quarto Dutch paper printed with their name and date. We are told that the King and his family purchased one.

Our hardy ancestors held their last great Frost Fair on the Thames in 1814, when after a week of dense freezing fog, great blocks of ice jammed against the piers of London Bridge. The ice was firm enough to hold a Gay Fair. By 2nd February streets of stalls, roundabouts, drinking booths and printing presses were all plying their trade and in full swing. However the celebrations were short lived. On 5th February rain fell and a sudden thaw set in, ominous cracks appeared in the ice and spread very rapidly, the floes began to float downstream and bore the booths away before many of the stallholders could salvage their wares.

In spite of many sheep being lost that winter, several of the West Country fairs reported the largest number of sheep ever at their autumn sales.

In the 1870s the destruction of the old London Bridge which acted as a partial dam and the building of the embankment made the prospect of future frost fairs unlikely - that is unless we get a prolonged period of extremely cold weather.

I wonder if this year will turn out to be severe enough to be recorded for posterity and for us to hold another Frost Fair.

189 February Nursery Rhymes
'NURSERY RHYMES AND THE TRUTH BEHIND THEM'

MOST of us were brought up on them; we have passed them onto our children, they in turn have taught them to their children - the nursery rhymes that we learnt at our mother's knee.

In early times they were so common that people were reluctant to write them down in expensive books that only a few could read - and they knew them by heart anyway.

It is therefore difficult to discover their true beginnings but one thing is for sure, the majority were originally destined for adult ears. It was because children were treated as adults in miniature that parents had no qualms about letting their offspring hear and repeat the bawdy songs, jokes and street cries of everyday life.

Over half our nursery rhymes are over two hundred years old and a quarter were known before the 1600s. They are a collection of easily remembered poems about courtship, conduct and counting methods, love ballads and political lampoonery, riddles and conundrums, amongst many other subjects. Nor are they unique to our country or culture.

Identical equivalents are to be found in most languages. The first small book of nursery rhymes was published in France around 1700, ten years later 'Mother Goose's Melodies' was produced in America, followed in England in 1744 by 'Tom Thumbs Pretty Songs'. They were also printed as penny song sheets, incorporated into ballads and referred to in stage plays. But more and more they became an aid to teaching children, a methodical way to learn the letters of the alphabet, the counting of numbers and to achieve a rhythmic coordination of movement and muscles.

Now, after the posturing, let us get down to practicalities. 'One, two, buckle my shoe," teaches the progression of numerals up to thirty although most now only go up to twenty; it was also one of many rhymes used for skipping and counting out. 'A is for archer' etc. not only teaches the letters of the alphabet but also the occupations of people and what they did or wore.

In cold weather hands could be warmed by playing the very ancient, 'Pat-a-cake, pat-a-cake, bakers man'. One of the earliest I remember was 'One a penny, two a-penny. Hot

cross buns' when the players hands were placed alternatively on top of one another, the bottom one withdrawn and placed on top of the pile, a game that became faster and faster as the child learned what to do.

Playing 'Here's the church and here's the steeple' can be very amusing when done properly. Almost identical hand movements are used when reciting 'Here are the ladies knives and forks'. Equally as fascinating are the 'Two little dicky birds sat upon a wall' when Peter and Paul disappear then re-appear again. Tongue twisters such as 'Peter Piper' demanded concentration, developed pronunciation and often produced exasperation! They were also recommended as a cure for hiccups! Some rhymes had a sinister side to their story such as 'Who killed cock robin?' or the second part of 'Oranges and Lemons' - 'Here comes a chopper to chop off your head', when the boy or girl 'caught' has to decide whose side to join for the final tug of war. Originally only those on the victor's side would have survived!

It is thought that some counting out games are relics of ancient ways of choosing sacrificial victims. 'Eena, meena, mina, mo' is certainly very similar to early methods of counting sheep. Another may be 'Hickory Dickory Dock'. When this was first recited there would have been no hands or even a dial on the clock, as is incorrectly illustrated in childrens' books today. The clock would have been a bell - it's no wonder the mouse ran down when the bell struck one. Meanwhile the misfortunes of the 'Three blind mice' were not only known about but also being sung as a round probably as far back as Tudor times.

The fortune of 'Little Jack Horner' came to common knowledge and ridicule when as a steward to Richard Whiting, the last Abbot of Glastonbury, who was fearful of his future and that of his monastery at the dissolution, sent him with the deeds of twelve manors concealed in a crust-capped pie to King Henry VIII.

On the way Jack Horner is related to have lifted the crust and removed the deeds of the manor of Mells in Somerset where his descendants still live - quite a plum!

'Sing a song of six-pence' is said by many to have come from that period. The pocket full of rye was the tithal tribute to the church after the grain had been sold, and four and twenty blackbirds represented the now darkened and doomed hours of the monasteries. The maid was a sinner of the former religion, a nun, and the blackbird that pecked off her nose was the devil reaching for her soul. Meanwhile the King (Henry VIII) was counting the money he had gained from the monastic coffers and the Queen in the parlour eating bread and honey was one of his six wives on honeymoon?

'Hark, hark the dogs do bark, the beggars are coming to town' may well have stemmed from the rich Catholics, the monks and nuns who were turned out of office. They had to beg for a living wearing whatever clothes they had on at the time, 'some in rags and some in tags and some in silken gowns.'

'Little boy blue' was almost certainly a political lampooning of Cardinal Wolsey who fell from favour. He was the son of butcher in Ipswich and as a young lad would have been sent to mind his father's stock, a monotonous task during which he fell asleep allowing the sheep to wander into the meadow destined for hay and the cows into the growing corn.

'Mary. Mary. quite contrary' may well have been Mary Queen of Scots. The dress given to her by her first husband, the Dauphin of France, had cockleshell docorations. The silver bells were the Catholic call to prayer at the mass and her pretty maids all in a row were Mary's - Beaton, Seaton, Fleming, Livingstone and Carmichael.

An alternative source refers to Our Lady's Convent of the Blessed Virgin Mary with its silver sanctus bells. The cockleshells in this case were the badges worn by pilgrims who had visited St James' shrine at Compostella in northern Spain. The pretty maids all in a row - were they the novice nuns?

'Goosey goosey gander' can be attributed to either of two terms of extreme ecclesiastical turmoil. That of Henry VIII and his daughters Mary & Elizabeth, or more probably Cromwell's Puritanical Period. In either case the goose stepping soldiers would search private premises for priests practising the forbidden faith. They often found their secret hiding places called Priests' holes under the floorboards or behind panelling, especially in the lady's bed chamber. Because the elderly priest would not confess to the new faith he was considered evil and in league with the devil - symbolised by the left leg (sinister side) - they threw him down the stairs which in reality meant they incarcerated him in the dungeons.

The pig that was stolen by 'Tom, Tom the piper's son' was not a live pig but a small pig-shaped sweetmeat sold by street hawkers called Pig Pye men in the 1700-1800s. Their cry was 'A long tailed pig or a short tailed pig, or a pig without any tail. A boar pig or a sow pig, or a pig with a curly tail. Take hold of the tail and eat off his head. And then you'll be sure the hog pig is dead'. As a salutory warning to others Tom was soundly beaten on his bottom.

There are two Royal suspects that fit the 'Georgie Porgie' rhyme. According to tradition the first was the amorous Charles II and the second was George I who lived with his mistress after divorcing his wife in 1694.

'The old woman that lived in a shoe' or as we might put it nowadays 'on a shoestring' could have been Queen Caroline the wife of George II who had eight children. Or it could equally well have fitted any large family as the shoe was the symbol of feminine fertility.

Perhaps the most quoted nursery rhyme is 'Mary had a little lamb' which was written in 1830 to recall a true incident in America. There are many adaptations of this, the most popular continues 'She also had a bear. I've often seen her little lamb, but I've never seen her bear'.

Sung to a french tune 'Baa, baa, black sheep' refers to the export tax placed on wool as long ago as 1275. The eight o'clock curfew, when fires were compulsorily covered is highlighted in 'Wee Willie Winkie'. The old word used to encourage children to close their eyes and go to sleep was bye-byes (sleep-sleep) - mother sang a lullaby(e) to lull them to sleep.

'Bye baby bunting' was an ancient term of endearment for a plump child who would soon be having a meal of rabbit broth and was warmed in clothes of its fur, as were a great many country children in bygone days when rabbits were regarded as a poor man's perk.

From America we also imported 'Rock a bye baby on the tree top'. It derived from the custom of the Red Indians to fasten their children in birch bark cradles suspended like hammocks from the branches of the trees which allowed the wind to gently rock them to sleep. The tune to which it is usually sung is a variant of 'Lilliburlero'.

Finally, one of my favounites is a riddle, see if you can work out the answer: 'Two legs sat on three legs, with one leg in his hand. In came four legs. ran away with one leg. Do you understand? Up jumped two legs, picked up three legs, threw it at four legs and got one leg back in his hand'.

Answer. A man sitting on a stool eating a leg of lamb - and his dog.

190 March Folklore of Flowers
'PART OF NATURE'S GREAT BEAUTY'

Whether they are fact or fiction, hidden behind the origin of many of our popular plants and flowers are some lovely legends. Some contain stories of how they came into existence, why they were so called, and when they changed their colours.   Others explain their alternative names or the uses to which they were put that you may never have realised before.

Because the SNOWDROP is white and is in bloom on the 'Feast of the Purification of the Blessed Virgin Mary' (2nd February), it became a symbol of purity and was used to decorate churches on that day, also known as 'Candlemas'. Perhaps that is why country people called them 'Fairy Lanterns', whilst religiously it was known as the 'Fair Maid of February'.

Legend has it that when Adam and Eve were evicted from the Garden of Eden it turned very cold and started snowing. To cheer them up, wherever the snowflakes settled on the ground they were transformed into little white flowers 'Snowdrops' and wherever Eve's tears fell they became white lilies.

Which leads us nicely on to the 'Lenten Lily', the DAFFODIL. This flower was originally white but Persephone, the daughter of the corn goddess, fell asleep whilst wearing a wreath of lilies on her head. Pluto, the God of the Underworld, captured her and carried her off in his chariot. Some of the lilies fell from her crown and with his hot touch turned to gold.

These golden flowers lined the banks of the river 'Acheron' that flowed into hell, they delighted the spirits of the departed who called them 'asphodels'. They thus became the symbol of death and were widely grown on graves.

During ancient spring rites, human sacrifices were decorated with them. In England they were known as 'AFFODILS' and in Wales 'Ceninpeder' which means the 'Leek of St Peter' which is why the Welsh national emblems are jointly a leek and a daffodil.

The CROCUS is dedicated to St Valentine and once upon a time its dried petals were made into love potions.

'Echo' was a nymph, who in punishment for her misdemeanours, was only able to repeat what others had just said. She was in love with NARCISSUS but as he did not return her love she pined away until only her voice remained. The reason he did not heed her advances was that he had fallen in love with a water nymph whom he saw every time he looked into a pool, never realising it was his own reflection.

One day he leant too far, slipped in and was drowned. When the water nymphs came looking for his body, all they could find was the strong smelling, white flower which ever since has been called 'Narcissus' after him. The Greek translation means 'to stiffen' possibly because of its narcotic effect on anyone who inhales too much of its scent.

Both the Narcissus and the POPPY are dedicated to 'Ceres' the goddess of corn. 'IRIS' the Goddess of the rainbow, from whose roots is made the calming 'Calamine', was married to 'Zephyr', the west wind.

'ANEMONE' a nymph of the woods fell in love with him, but his wife was having none of it. She banished 'Anemone', who pined away and died of a broken heart. However, 'Venus' brought her back to life as a flower which would bloom every spring. Sadly 'Anemone' was forsaken by 'Zephyr' but was adopted by 'Boreas', the north wind which is why it is so often in evidence during March and April when she is in flower.

Fairies were believed to use 'anemones' to shelter in when it rained and ' the North wind both blow'. They creep into the flowers and pull the petals closely around them to keep them warm and dry, which is why the flowers always close when it rains. Another plant beloved of the fairies is 'HONESTY', whose old name was Moonwort, they use the round silver seed pods for money when they meet at their markets on moonlit nights. The plant used to be taken internally as a remedy against moon madness. Incidentally the name of the Goddess of all blooming plants and fertility is 'Flora' which now means 'flowers' - that should spread a little happiness!

'Zephyr', the west wind, was quite a character and comes into yet another legend. He was playing quoits with 'Apollo' and 'HYACINTH', the son of a Spartan King. 'Zephyr' blew too hard, the quoit struck 'Hyacinth' on the head and killed him, whereupon the Gods caused a flower with weeping bells to grow where he had died - the 'Hyacinth'.

The Latin name for 'BLUEBELL' is Endymium. He was a handsome shepherd boy on Mount Latmos who was loved by the moon. He wished for eternal youth but in granting his request the Gods decreed that he lies forever in 'eternal sleep', but every night he is 'kissed' by the moon.

Before the 16th Century the 'Bluebell' was called the Harebell. To add an additional link to the legend the hare was believed to be the messenger of the Moon and associated with 'OESTRE' the Goddesss of the Srping (Easter) which was thought to be why hares act so unusually during March!

A large number of plants take their names, unusual patterns, colours or other attributes from the early days of Christianity.

SAIN FOIN or holy hay is a vetch that was believed to have lined the manger where Jesus was laid. The white markings on the leaves of the sow or 'MILK THISTLE' were formed when the plant was splashed with the Virgin Mary's milk. She dried her baby's clothes on a spiky 'LAVENDER' bush to dry. The bush tried to scent the clothes and for its efforts was rewarded with a fragrant scent and blue flowers, still used to perfume clothing. A somewhat similar story is told of the 'ROSEMARY' whose flowers are blue because the Virgin Mary dried her cloak on a bush and the dye ran out! Its fragrance is very soothing and will induce both love making and sleep - probably in that order. It was thought the bush would only grow to a height of six feet three inches and live for thirty three years,the height and age which Jesus attained whilst on earth. In some countries it is known as 'The Pilgrims Flower' because Mary rested in its shade with Joseph and Jesus on their flight into Egypt.

'LILIES' are dedicated to the Virgin Mary, they symbolise motherhood, sincerity and common sense, when Jesus hung on the cross the lily hung her head and wept, which is why there is always a tiny tear at the base of the flower.

The smaller 'LILIES OF THE VALLEY' sprang up where Mary's tears fell at the foot of the cross whilst the tips of the petals of the DAISY were tinged pink by the drops of Jesus' blood.

The most famous crucifixion emblem of all is the 'PASSION FLOWER' so named by 16th century Spanish missionaries to South Africa. The leaf symbolises the spear; the tendrils the scourges; the column of the ovary - the pillar of the cross; the five anthers - Jesus' wounds; the filaments within the flower - the Crown of thorns; the calyx - the gloria; the white tint - purity; the blue tint - heaven; the five petals and the five sepals - the ten commandments and also the ten disciples excluding Peter who denied him and Judas who betrayed him.

In France the PANSY is also known as 'Three pretty faces under one hood'. It once had a scent sweeter than violets. People trampled the corn to gather it and so much corn was wasted that there was a famine and many people perished. The Pansy prayed for her scent to be taken away so th.0.000at people would not ruin the corn and suffer the consequences. Her prayer was granted and so in France the Pansy, the 'Three faces under one hood' is now called the 'TRINITY FLOWER'.

'GILLYFLOWERS' or 'CARNATIONS' were worn in garlands by both Greeks and Romans on festive occasions. In England to wear one was a sign that the person was already betrothed. The flowers were once used to spice wine at majestic events and may well have formerly been called 'CORONATION'!

It has a connection in legend with the 'CHRYSANTHEMUM', which was known 2,500 years ago. In Japan it became the personal emblem of the MIKADO, only he and the nobility were allowed to grow or wear it. Their flag of the Rising Sun was originally a chrysanthemum, their national flower. How it obtained so many petals is explained in the legend that a beautiful girl who loved her husband very much was told by the Gods he would live for as many years as a flower had petals. She searched and searched for such a flower and eventually found a 'carnation'. To extend the length of their happiness she cut every petal into very thin strips - and created the 'CHRYSANTHEMUM'.

When flowers were first formed the 'CONVOLVULUS' had a great friend. They embraced and twisted around each other whenever the wind blew upon them. One day there arose a great storm which blew them apart and blinded Convolvulus. From that day to this it has wandered the world in search of its companion. When it finds another plant it entwines it as if hoping to find its long lost friend. This is why the 'CONVOLVULUS' is used as a symbol to entwine the bonds of love and marriage. Its common name is 'BINDWEED'.

There are at least two legends about my final flower. A lovely young lady and her lover were strolling beside a fast flowing river and saw some beautiful blue flowers growing on the bank - just out of reach. As he stretched to gather them he toppled in, but as he was being swept away he managed to throw the flowers to his sweetheart with the words 'FORGET-ME-NOT'. That is a fairly recent German legend, this one is much, much older.

At the beginning of time an angel was sent with a message to a holy man living on earth. As he flew down he saw a beautiful girl plaiting blue flowers in her hair. He descended, made love to her and they lived happily together.

After many years the angel remembered he had not delivered the message. He flew back to Heaven to ask forgiveness but found the gates were closed. Eventually, the Arch-Angel Gabriel appeared and said 'You must people the earth with children of the sky before you can bring a daughter of the earth into heaven'. He did not understand the message and flew back to earth and asked his beautiful bride if she could explain it. 'Yes' she said taking some of the blue flowers from her hair. 'These lovely little blue flowers reflect the colour of heaven and are the children of the sky'. So the angel and his bride wandered the earth and planted 'FORGET-ME-NOTS' in every country.

When their task was completed the angel took his bride in his arms, carried her up to heaven and entered through the open gates.

What a lovely story that is, and quite recently and quite by accident I came across this poem:

> The little flower said in trembling tones,
> With sweet and gentle grace,
> 'Dear God the name Thou gavest me, Alas I have forgot'.
> Then kindly looked the Father down,
> And said 'FORGET-ME-NOT'.

191 April Dogs Life
'TAILS FROM MAN'S BEST FRIEND'

Although dogs are regarded as 'Man's most faithful friend' there are probably many aspects of their background that, like me, you have accepted without ever giving them a second thought. Some explanations are surprisingly simple, but because they are part of our everyday language we never bother to probe beneath the surface to find the facts, so here goes.

Dogs are thought to have derived from two main sources, the grey wolf and the jackal. Both of them are pack animals. When a quarry was killed every member tucked in avidly. The faster they ate the more meat they obtained, and those that ate slowly soon starved, which is why dogs still bolt their food.

Before they lay down to rest in the reeds, rushes or long grass they turned round several times to bend and flatten the stems to make themselves a comfortable bed, as they still do. When out hunting they 'bay' to keep the pack together, howling is an ancestral way of attracting the rest of the pack, and they bury their bones to prevent others stealing them.

Dogs can go for long periods without either food or water and as they manufacture their own vitamin C they do not need fresh fruit or vegetables.

Neolithic man domesticated dogs because they hunted in the same way that he did. Dogs could be tamed and trained to increase his ability to track, trap and kill his prey. Greeks used them as weapons of war and five thousand years ago the Egyptians treated them as Gods.

They named Sirius the dog star because of its faithful warning appearance just before the Nile overflowed in full flood every year. The ancients believed that it was the extra heat given off by this 'Dog-star', which when added to the heat of the sun caused the six weeks of 'Dog days' from July 3rd to August 11th which made so many dogs go mad at that time of the year.

The entrance to Hades on the far side of the river Styx was said to be guarded by the vicious many headed dog 'Cerberus'. In the Old testament Jacob, Job and David all used dogs to protect their flocks of sheep from thieves, robbers and wolves.

Because of the strength and savagery of these guard dogs they were declared 'unclean' by Moses and classed as scavengers not worthy of a serious mention, and in the New Testament dogs licked the sores of Lazarus as he lay at the rich mans gate, because of this we have the expression 'Dirty Dog'. Alexander the Great and later the Romans used heavily built, ugly and stubborn mastiffs for fighting. They were protected by body armour and wore a heavy spiked collar. They were described as 'terrible and frightful to behold', being trained to wound and kill by harsh maltreatment.

The earliest records of dogs being used to guard sheep in England was in 300BC. In

Tudor times a scraggy dog called a 'cur' moved cattle along the droving trails to the main centres of population. The Welsh equivalent was the short legged Corgi ('dwarf dog') which would nip at their heels to get them moving. Being so small the resultant kick would pass way over the dog's head.

The breed which developed to herd sheep was called a Collie, named after a now extinct black faced-sheep. Sheepdogs rapidly developed a natural instinct to scour the hills and dales on command to round up the flock, guard them at night, stop them straying or stampeding and bring them safely home. They were also excellent in discovering sheep lost in snowstorms or buried in snowdrifts. Farmers in the French region of Alsace used a wolf-like sheepdog which we now know as the Alsatian or German Shepherd dog.

Because of the element of competitive spirit in them the first sheepdog trials were held at Bala, North Wales in 1873. Most modern working sheepdogs can trace their lineage back to the exceptional 'Old Hemp' of the late 1800s. In common with many countrymen I found it very amusing when a few years ago the TV show, 'One Man and His Dog' championship was won by a young girl and her three legged dog.

Probably the hardiest dogs are Huskies who endure the harshest extremes of arctic weather when they pull Eskimo sledges over the snow.

A close runner up searched the snowy Alpine passes for lost or buried pilgrims seeking refuge in the Monastery of St Bernard which was established in AD 962. Its acute sense of smell could trace a human scent up to three miles away, or buried several feet under an avalanche. It would dig down to them, huddle up beside them to keep them warm or guide them to the monastery. Strapped to its back it had bread and blankets - and around its neck a barrel of brandy! Of course, you will have guessed by now that it was the Saint Bernard.

Another dog of religious origin is the Tibetan spaniel, a small dog trained to herd sheep, guard the monastery gates and turn the prayer wheels during religious services. They were small enough to hide in the wide sleeves of the monks robes where they acted as a hot water bottle in the depths of winter.

In England ladies took 'lap dogs' to church for the same purpose, larger dogs also often accompanied them. Any who started fighting or misbehaving were forcibly ejected by a special dog warden known as a 'knocknobbler'. He brandished a whip or used a pair of extending 'lazy' tongs. One church in Wales had a small door specifically for their removal. In larger country houses there once existed a dog known as a 'Turnspit' whose task it was to walk the wheel which drove the pulley to turn the spit that roasted the meat in front of the fire. Historically to be found at the foot of the stairs is a dog-gate, a relic of the days when dogs guarded the downstairs rooms of the great houses at night but were prevented from going upstairs into the bedrooms.

Probably the most pampered was the Pekingese. Up to the 14C they were the favourite of the Chinese Emperors and they lived a life of luxury. They shared his throne, held titles such as dukes and princes and were given sizeable salaries. They were cared for by servants, bathed and perfumed daily, lay on silk cushions and were carried on magnificent covered couches called palaquins which were borne by four or six men. They were known as 'Lion dogs' and considered sacred, anyone who maltreated or tried to steal them was severely punished.

A dog which often causes a smile is the French Poodle especially when it has just had its fancy 'Lion' haircut. But there is an important reason behind this removal. Its German name, Puddlehund - 'dog which splashes in water' - gives a good clue, the shaving of its hindquarters allows the dog to swim faster while the rings of fur left on the legs help to prevent rheumatism of the joints, and the pom-pom at the end of its tail indicates its position when swimming submerged.

Another breed which loves water is the Newfoundland. It has an instinct for saving lives and being an extremely strong swimmer it will haul small boats to the shore by gripping the tow-rope with its jaws. Spaniels also work well on land or in the water, and they originated in Spain. From about 1400AD they were used to flush - or 'spring' - game from cover for falconers, hence Springer spaniels.

The busy shorter legged Cocker spaniels were so called because of their ability to send woodcock into flight. For the last couple of hundred years or so they have been classed as gundogs. Others in that group include the Setter who crouches and 'sets' its quarry, the Pointer who stands rigid on sniffing the airborne scent of game, be it pheasant, partridge, grouse or quail.

The Labrador Retriever has a fantastic memory of where shot birds have fallen and will tenderly fetch them back at the end of the shoot without any damage. They have such a soft mouth that when collecting hens' eggs I often used to give one to my Labrador to carry home, and she never broke it. She showed her pleasure by wagging her strong tail which acted like a rudder in her rear. Dogs cannot smile for if they did they would bare their teeth, which to them is a sign of aggression.

The dog which developed the strongest sense of smell is of course the Bloodhound. Its nose is so sensitive it can track a single scent several days old.

Dogs which chased or 'hounded' their prey - deer, otter, fox and badger - were termed hounds. Beagles and Bassets hunted hares and rabbits and were usually followed on foot. The dog best known for coursing is the Greyhound which can clock-up speeds of forty miles per hour. It still chases an electric-hare around the racing stadium. A now extinct breed for

hares was the Harrier. Equivalent hunting dogs from Northern Europe are the Great Dane and, from Russia, the Borzoi, a graceful running wolf-hound. The German hound bred to 'badger' the badger was the Dachshund.

Generally any dog which went to ground after its prey was termed a Terrier from the French and Latin word for earth.

The spotted pudding dog or Dalmatian came from Yugoslavia, it was trained to run under the carriages of the rich to protect its occupants from footpads or highwaymen. It enjoys the company of horses and can cover long distances at considerable speed.

The dog identified with the indominatable British spirit of 'dogged' determination and courage is the Bulldog. It was at first destined to hunt wild boars but when they became hunted to extinction the dogs were used by butchers to catch cattle, which they did by hanging on to their nose. They became known as 'Butcher dogs' but when a law was introduced that compelled all bulls to be baited before slaughter, this was the ideal dog to do it, so it became the Bulldog. And while I am on the subject, do you know why there are studs around a dog's collar? They are a relic of bygone days when they were sharp spikes, put there to prevent the dog being throttled by a bear hug when bear-baiting.

And even if you can't teach an old dog new tricks, there are many fresh pursuits that existing breeds can exploit. Guide dogs for the blind, mine detectors, drug and bomb sniffers and many more, all in addition to being 'man's most faithful friend'.

192 May Farm Sales
'A GREAT BUT SAD OCCASION IN THE COUNTRY'

Among those of us who live and work in the countryside a FARM SALE is considered a social occasion.

Although for the farmer and his family it is the culmination of a lifetime of labour on the land, for the rest of the community it is a chance to step through the gates and see everything first hand instead of looking over the hedge.

Like farmers, 'Farm Sales' vary widely. From the smart and tidy, up-to-date, almost everything new enterprise, to the other extreme where the owner has kept everything from day one, even though it is never used, because it might come in handy someday. Most 'Farm Sales' fall somewhere in between.

About an hour before the start, a slow trickle of expectant bargain hunters follow the 'To the Sale' signs and arrive at the farm. This influx increases almost to a deluge as others, having hurriedly finished milking, feeding and mucking out on their own farms, turn up in anything from expensive 4 x 4s to old bangers, pick-up trucks or tractors.

The dealers and hauliers with their specialised vehicles have difficulty getting through the rows of vehicles parked haphazardly for several hundred yards on either side of the farm and on both sides of the road.

The gateway and tracks leading to the pasture put aside for parking is already becoming a quagmire after overnight rain. Rather surprisingly to anyone who is not accustomed to country ways a wet day usually brings more buyers than a dry one, simply because as farmers cannot get on with their work outside at home, when it is wet they take an hour or two off to attend a sale.

A few prospective purchasers walk up and down the rows of neatly laid out paraphernalia, boxes of bits and pieces, small tools, implements and tractors. Each lot numbered with an oval shaped white ticket attached with a dab of very sticky glue.

Groups of farmers and friends gather to discuss the weather, market prices, their problems and any local scandal that happens to come to hand.

A queue begins to form at the hot drinks and hot dog stall run by the outside caterer. The aroma wafts through the adjoining sheds where others stand huddled out of the rain and the cold wind. Occasionally the nose twitches at slightly more unsavoury smells - stale milk, cow manure, silage, chlorine and iodine, impregnated into the clothing of those attending.

A few minutes past the official time a hand bell rings to signify the start of the sale. Almost as if by magic the scattered crowd coagulate into a seething, jostling mass around the auctioneer and his clipboard clutching assistant.

The auctioneer briefly explains the reasons behind the sale and the rules applying to the purchases, then the buying begins in earnest. With a rapidity that defies understanding to the unaccustomed ear, the auctioneer identifies the lot number, the purpose of the item and gives an idea of how much he expects it to fetch in his opening sentence.

He then starts taking bids with such a rapid succession of comments and quips that he often lures the unwary into paying more than they had intended, some things more than it was worth and occasionally to have bought a new one would have been cheaper! There is such a tightly packed crowd that it is difficult for the uninitiated to know what is being sold and many an inexperienced bidder finds he has purchased the wrong lot when he goes to pay his bill at the 'office' afterwards.

The auctioneer's frequent requests to 'stand away from the lots please, let the dog see the rabbit', falls on deaf ears to those who know the system and intend buying.

Bidding is an art form in itself. From his immense experience the auctioneer knows how each individual bids. A nod of the head, a flick of the finger, the raising of the catalogue, a wink or a touch is noted even out of the corner of his eye. The bid is accepted and a higher price is requested, if obtained the auctioneer returns to the previous bidder to raise the price higher or shake his head, until the limit is reached and the item is 'knocked down' to the highest bidder with a tap of his stick on the lot.

Occasionally a bid is missed, the complainant is counteracted by the comment, 'you must shout out if I don't see you'. The auctioneer and his assistant booking lots, seldom forget a face. Each purchaser is identified with a kind of code, sometimes it is their full name but more often it is their initials 'R.R' - the name of their farm, village or temporary nickname they have acquired from a purchase earlier in the sale. It is rare that either he or his clerk makes a mistake.

Because everything has to go, any item that doesn't raise a bid may be included with the next lot in the hopes that the following purchaser will remove it. At a good sale there is always a constant flow of banter between the auctioneer and his audience.

A purchase going for a pound or so, followed by an expensive item, will lead to some wag shouting 'stand on' (an expression which means same price for this one) which sends a titter around the crowd. On selling some old seized up piece of machinery the auctioneer will say 'It worked the last time it was used', or if he doesn't really know what it is 'I'm selling it as seen because I've never seen one like it before'.

Any items that don't get an immediate response are quickly knocked down to an itinerant scrap dealer, even if he isn't there, to keep up the momentum of the sale for there's nothing that drags the prices down as quickly as a slow turnover of items. However, nowadays there are many new uses for old items.

Horse ploughs, cultivators and scarifiers are brought for public house car parks. Hay cratches can be affixed to outside walls and filled with summer flowering plants, whilst stone feed and water troughs, iron drinking bowls and earthenware chimney pots decorate the gardens of suburbia.

As at most sales the item belongs to the purchaser at the fall of the hammer, so on an open field any valuable small pieces are picked up by the buyer straight away and carried around or carted to the car. 'Stand back please' warns the auctioneer over the clamour of conversation as the tractor is started up, moved a yard or two forwards then reversed again to prove that it works.

Next it is a wander around isolated items in the farmyard for lots that have been left on site, such as hen-houses, piles of firewood, electric motors and dairy equipment. Surplus household furniture is sold from the porch or in an outbuilding as the farmhouse rooms couldn't possibly accommodate such a crowd.

Then it is the turn of the livestock, hens, pigs, sheep, horses and cattle. Up to now the retiring farmer and his staff have not been too upset by the disposal of dead-stock - the implements. But livestock - living animals - have a much higher sentimental attachment especially when you have looked after them for the whole of their life.

Many a time I have seen hardened farmers, their faces weathered by years of exposure to the elements, with tears streaming down their cheeks as they run their favourite workhorses up and down to display them to the onlookers. Or stood on the covered rostrum with the auctioneer as he sold the cows that they had milked twice every day of their productive life.

The farmer knows only too well that the purchaser will never hold them in such high esteem as he has. All he can hope for is that they either go to a good home or that their end will be quick and painless.

The last animal goes 'under the hammer' and is sold, the buyers queue to pay their dues at the 'office' where reality overcomes enthusiasm and the remark is often heard, 'Cor, I didn't pay that much for it did I, how on earth am I going to explain that to the missus when she sees my accounts'.

Meanwhile the livestock are being loaded into the lorries, the small and medium sized objects are packed into car boots or onto roof racks, tractors roll up to take away the larger implements.

By dusk only a few items remain in each of the rows, they too will be collected in the next day or two until eventually only one pile will remain - the one the auctioneer couldn't get a bid for and put it with the next.

After tea the farmer wanders around wondering how it happened that the woodworm riddled butter churn he almost burned on the bonfire made a small fortune and why the implement he paid a small fortune for at another farm sale only a year ago went for peanuts, a real bargain for some lucky bidder.

As he strolls through the strangely silent, deserted farmyard, the empty sheds echo with an eerie feeling he has never experienced before, no implements, no tractors, no animals and above all no clutter to absorb the sounds.

A lifetime of accumulations disposed of in a day, that's what a 'Farm Sale' means to a farmer and there are very few who can shoulder the change without shedding a silent tear. But life goes on, within a few months the recently RETIRED farmer will be so busy he will be wondering how on earth he ever found the time to farm - at least that's what happened to me!

193 June Gardens
'GARDENS THROUGH THE CENTURIES'

If you should happen to visit the church at the top of my garden, standing somewhere on the greensward between the porch and yew tree is a lovely old wooden garden seat. Carved into its back rail are four lines of a famous poem.

> 'The kiss of the sun for pardon,
> The song of the birds for mirth,
> You are nearer God's heart in a garden,
> Than anywhere else on earth.'

With everything growing so rapidly I thought this would be an appropriate time to delve into the development of the garden.

According to Genesis, the first book of the Bible, 'The Lord God planted a garden, eastward of Eden'. It contained every kind of tree pleasant to the sight and good for food, and therein grew the mysterious tree of life and the knowledge of good and evil. There was also a river which flowed through and watered Paradise. Today we would be more likely to describe it as a delightful park, for the word 'Eden' actually means pleasant and delightful.

Probably the most magnificent garden built by man was the one King Nebuchadnezzar built for his wife, who was weary of the dreary flat plains of Babylon and longed for her Median Hills. It was so majestic it became one of the seven wonders of the ancient world - 'The Hanging Gardens of Babylon'.

It covered about four acres near the palace, was some 300 feet high (approx 100 metres), had arched walls 75 feet thick and high (25 metres). Above was a square garden 400 feet each way (125 metres) rising in a series of terraces.

It grew groves of trees of a great size, was perfumed with a profusion of flowers and had built-in banqueting halls. It was watered from a reservoir at the top which was filled from the river Euphrates by an Archimedian screw driven by slaves.

A few centuries later, in 550BC, King Cyrus of Persia had gardens of short cropped flowers, shrubs and greenery laid out in intricate patterns indicative of Persian carpets and in full view of his palace.

The Greeks, too, had gardens of flowers, fruit and vegetables with trees for shelter. The Egyptians developed irrigation to a high degree with hand and donkey powered water wheels to enable them to maintain their rather stiff and formal gardens with high hedges of thorny shrubs, roses and wild pomegranates. Their main purpose was to provide shade from the incessant sun, and they also had roof gardens. All were tended and watered by their slaves.

The Garden of Gethsemane, at the foot of the Mount of Olives, was only three quarters of a mile from Jerusalem, just over the brook Kedron. It was a public garden where olive trees grew, it also had an oil press. It was used as a gathering place during religious festivities, whilst in its quieter moments it became a refuge, a place of silence, solitude and devotional retirement. In its stony outcrops were constructed tombs for the burial of rich and prominent people.

When the Romans invaded Britain they introduced the gardening style of their homeland, which slowly superceded Celtic customs, formal geometric shapes surrounded by hedges to keep it warmer and within which grew fruit trees trained to grow at an angle - pleached and espalier. They had shaped evergreen trees which we now call topiary, a few flowers for utility not beauty, several vegetables including peas and beans which for reasons they did not understand made the following crops produce more. We now know that they are producers of nitrogen.

From their houses and gardens they had fine views of the countryside. All this changed when they withdrew and the continental raiding parties became established as Anglo-Saxon farmers. They allowed their hens and pigs to roam freely and lived off their meat rather than garden grown vegetables.

However, with our next invaders, the Normans from France in 1066, gardens began to flourish once more. They grew great beds of onions and garlic. Water meadows increased fertility and grew better crops, mill ponds produced fish and eels for food. Pigs were used to control the spread of bracken.

The increasing number of monks and nuns grew herbs for health, installed fish ponds and grew grapes for wine. Beekeeping improved the pollination and therefore the yield for their orchards, the grass under the trees was kept under control by sheep and deer.

By 1300AD there were about three thousand special enclosures for deer hunting, a forerunner of our later parkland. As people became richer and independent they increasingly grew their own vegetables, herbs and flowers.

By Elizabethan times gardens were once again the vogue. But with a characteristic difference. Each area, whether it was a flower, vegetable or herb patch, was likely to be enclosed by a low trellis or a short cropped interlacing box or yew hedge. Overlooking these patterned 'knot' gardens were raised banks topped with turf, thyme, camomile and violets.

From them, not only could the complexity of the designs be enjoyed, but they also acted as vantage points when watching 'bowls' or 'club-ball' (an early form of cricket) being played on the scythe-cut grass. The art of topiary returned and an increasing interest in trees led to the formation of shady 'arbours'.

Large houses had smaller houses for use in the summer built in their gardens 'summerhouses'. Hedged 'mazes' became very popular.

During the 17th century many of the larger houses adopted a French design which aimed at very long avenues, having flowers in the foreground, rows of trees in the middle ground and a focal point of a church, a monument or a folly in the distance. This was called a 'parterre'.

Also on the scene was an exciting new flower, the tulip. So great was the enthusiasm for the unusual colours that some bulbs changed hands for vast sums of money.

In the mid and late 1700s, there arose a reaction to formal gardens. At the forefront was a designer who would view the scene and say, 'This has capabilities'. His name was Lancelot 'Capability' Brown.

He left his mark on over two hundred country estates by clearing hedges, walks and enclosed gardens to create a parkland scenery. Sweeping turf, accentuated by clumps of trees and wooded slopes, led the eye to lakes, gazebos, temples and bridges.

Whole villages were moved to improve the vista from mansions. Not even fencing for animals was allowed to impede the view as miles of ha-ha's were dug by an army of workers.

A hundred years later the cycle turned yet again and the formal flower beds returned to favour. Stimulated by the expansion of the Empire, plant collectors scavenged the four corners of the globe to bring back new varieties of trees, shrubs and flowers hitherto unknown.

The invention of the cylindrical lawn mower in 1830 meant that all and sundry could now have a grassed area that could be kept under control without scything the sod every week. Small areas were cut with a hand-pushed mower, while larger lawns used pony or donkey power. The animals were fitted with special overshoes so that their hoofs would not damage the turf.

Usually out of sight, somewhere behind the big house, was the walled vegetable garden. There a horde of gardeners grew all the fruit, vegetables and flowers needed to supply the kitchen throughout the year. Glasshouses, conservatories and orangeries were heated by coke boilers which needed constant attention in winter.

But just as the Hanging Gardens of Babylon and the exotic gardens of Egypt and the Roman Empire fell to rack and ruin when there were no slaves to tend them, so the slaughter of young men in the First world war heralded the decline of the heavily staffed 'Victorian' type of garden.

With the growth of towns and the increase in the number of kinds of houses, the vast majority with a garden, came an explosion in the demand for fruit and ornamental trees,

shrubs and flowers. At first these were grown on site from seed, then purchased from 'Market Gardens' and more recently from 'Garden Centres'.

Some years ago I read that there were over ten million gardeners in England. Unfortunately about a third of them consider gardening a chore, which seems such a shame, for gardening is one of the purest pleasures, recreating the countryside in miniature form.

The changes in gardening style and design are never abrupt. Each has its seeds in the past, its flowers in the present and its fruit in the future. All of which leads me to another verse written by the poetess Mrs Frances Gurney:

> 'And he who is the garden's friend,
> Groweth calm and wise
> And after death shall rise and tend
> His plot in Paradise!'

The life of man began in a garden - the Garden of Eden. Many of us may well finish up in a garden - a garden of remembrance. You can't get away from it, can you!

Countrywise One

Countrywise Two

Countrywise Three

Countrywise Four